THE

PUBLICATIONS

OF THE

Lincoln Record Society

FOUNDED IN THE YEAR

1910

VOLUME 55

FOR THE YEAR ENDING 31ST AUGUST, 1960

THE

BUILDING ACCOUNTS

OF

TATTERSHALL CASTLE

1434—1472

EDITED BY

W. DOUGLAS SIMPSON

O.B.E., D.LITT.

Librarian of the University of Aberdeen

PRINTED FOR

THE LINCOLN RECORD SOCIETY

BY

THE HEREFORD TIMES LIMITED, HEREFORD

1960

First published 1960

Reprinted in paperback 2010
Transferred to digital printing

A Lincoln Record Society publication with The Survey of Lincoln
published by The Boydell Press
PO Box 9, Woodbridge, Suffolk IP12 3DF, UK
and of Boydell & Brewer Inc.
668 Mt. Hope Avenue, Rochester NY 14620, USA
website: www.boydellandbrewer.com

ISBN 978-0-90150-389-3

A catalogue record for this title is available
from the British Library

This publication is printed on acid-free paper

Printed in Great Britain by
4edge Ltd, Hockley, Essex

PREFACE

The publication of this work has been inordinately delayed. This is partly due to my own ill-health and partly to various mishaps, of which the most spectacular is perhaps unique in the record of such undertakings. My house was invaded by a monkey, escaped from a travelling circus a mile or more away : and, in the fracas consequent on efforts to recapture it, some of the transcripts were so badly damaged that they had to be re-written !

To the Lincoln Record Society I am deeply indebted for the honour they have done me by undertaking the publication. Other due acknowledgements will be found on p. xxx : but here I cannot deny myself the pleasure of testifying to my enormous indebtedness to the Honorary Editor of the Society, Miss Kathleen Major. Not only has she carefully checked the transcripts against the original rolls, but her assistance in the translation and commentary has been invaluable : moreover, she has written the palæographical note at p. xxxii, and has prepared the Index of Persons and Places.

The blocks for the Illustrations, save Fig. 1, have been lent by Aberdeen University Library.

The foundation of all study of Tattershall must always be the sumptuous volume published under Lord Curzon's will by the late Mr. H. Avray Tipping in 1929. My indebtedness to this work will be obvious to all who read the following pages. No student of Lord Cromwell's Great Tower can afford to ignore the magnificent series of large-scale measured drawings which, in 1872, obtained for Mr. Fred H. Reed the silver medal of the R.I.B.A., and were published by him in the same year.

W. Douglas Simpson.

King's College, Old Aberdeen,
Easter, 1960

CONTENTS

LIST OF ILLUSTRATIONS

A BIBLIOGRAPHIC NOTE by David Stocker

Castle studies have developed greatly since Douglas Simpson wrote so interestingly in the introduction reprinted here (pages xi–xxix), and this note's purpose is to draw the attention of twenty-first century readers to some of the key publications that have developed Simpson's ideas about 'great towers' since he wrote in 1960. Briefly put, writing about Tattershall in the past half-century has followed the roller-coaster of discussion regarding great castles in England in general. Simpson himself was a member of a generation of castle scholars who had been through army training and who were influenced by their military experiences in both World Wars (Simpson himself was a veteran of WWI). Partly as a result, no doubt, they viewed even such apparently domestic buildings as Thornbury Castle and Ashby-de-la-Zouch with the eye of the military tactician.[1] One of the leaders of this generation, Michael Thompson, was himself greatly interested in Tattershall and wrote several pieces about it in the vein established by Simpson himself.[2]

But subsequent scholars have been more greatly influenced by economic and social history and by the work of archaeologists arriving at the castle gate with more complex anthropological perspectives.[3] Many such writers have questioned whether the military imperative, which was so fundamental to Simpson's generation, was quite as dominant in castle building as they presumed. Much more complex networks of influences on the design and appearance of castles have been explored, and such scholars suggest that our understanding of buildings such as Tattershall's great tower should be guided at least as much by their builders' interests in contemporary art and literature, politics and sociology, as by their personal insecurities or their skills in military engineering.

Although the debate over how we should best study castles is sometimes presented as a clash between two armed camps (especially, perhaps, by those with a military perspective!), in fact the orthodoxy of Simpson's day has become a wide spectrum of approaches. More conservative historians and art historians still write about castles in general;[4] and indeed about Tattershall in particular.[5] Such work has ensured that the questions originally posed by Simpson in 1960 regarding the military

1 W. D. Simpson, *Castles in England and Wales* (London, 1969), 160–2. R. Allen Brown's masterpiece, *English Medieval Castles* (London), had been first published in 1954 and set the standard for orthodox readings of castles, through numerous editions and reprintings, for the next 50 years; the most recent edition (Woodbridge, 2004) contains a valuable introduction by J. Coad.

2 M. W. Thompson, *The Decline of the Castle* (Cambridge, 1987); M. W. Thompson, *Tattershall Castle, Lincolnshire* (London: National Trust, 1974); M. W. Thompson, 'The architectural significance of the buildings works of Ralph, Lord Cromwell (1394–1456)', in A. Detsicas (ed.), *Collectanea Historica: Essays in Memory of Stuart Rigold* (Maidstone: Kent Archaeological Society, 1981), 55–62; M. W. Thompson, 'Tattershall Castle', *Archaeological Journal* 131 (1974), 334.

3 P. Dixon, 'The Donjon at Knaresborough: The Castle as Theatre', *Château Gaillard* 14 (1990), 121–39; N. J. G. Pounds, *The Medieval Castle in England and Wales: A social and political history* (Cambridge, 1990); D. Stocker, 'The Shadow of the General's Armchair', *Archaeological Journal* 149 (1992), 415–20; P. Dixon and B. Lott, 'The Courtyard and the Tower: contexts and symbols in the development of late medieval great houses', *Journal of the British Archaeological Association* 146 (1993), 93–101; P. Dixon, 'Design in Castle Building: the controlling of access to the lord', *Chateau Gaillard* 18 (1998), 47–57; M. Johnson, *Behind the Castle Gate: from Medieval to Renaissance* (London, 2002), especially ch. 3 where Tattershall is one of Johnson's critical studies; P. Marshall, 'The ceremonial function of the donjon in the twelfth century', *Château Gaillard* 20 (2002), 141–51; C. Coulson, *Castles in Medieval Society, Fortresses in England, France and Ireland in the central Middle Ages* (Oxford, 2003); P. Dixon, 'The Myth of the Keep', in G. Meirion-Jones, E. Impey and M. C. E. Jones (eds), *The Seigneurial Residence in Western Europe AD c.800–1600*, BAR (IS) 1088 (Oxford, 2002), 9–13; A. Wheatley, *The Idea of the Castle in Medieval England* (Woodbridge, 2004).

4 D. J. Cathcart King, *The Castle in England and Wales: An Interpretative History* (London, 1988); C. Platt, 'Revisionism in Castle Studies: A Caution', *Medieval Archaeology* 51 (2007), 83–102.

5 T. Avery, *Tattershall Castle, Lincolnshire* (London, 1997); J. Goodall, 'Tattershall Castle, Lincoln-

origins of the design for Tattershall's great tower continue to be debated. But whilst some writers adhere to more traditional stances, based in the tactics of warfare, such approaches are of less interest to a generation of archaeologists accustomed to setting their discoveries in the wider context of the contemporary landscape.[6] Tattershall has also benefited from consideration by archaeologists trying to see the castle within just such wider settings, and its development has been reinterpreted in the contexts, both of the hunting chase in which it was established, and relative to the town and college that was founded alongside it.[7] This more recent work on Tattershall has tended to draw attention away from the surviving great tower and towards phases of the castle's development about which less is known, but which were equally significant in the area's history.[8] Following consolidation work in 2003–4,[9] The National Trust itself commissioned a conservation plan for the whole castle, completed in 2009, which represents much the fullest statement presently available regarding the castle's history and fabric, incorporating some important new archival research on the later history of site.[10] In a separate recent development, the great tower has become a focus for important research into the dating of early brickwork, led by the Archaeo-science Laboratory at the University of Durham.[11]

Finally, work on documentary sources relevant to castle studies has also intensified since 1960. Most significantly perhaps, 1963 saw the publication of the medieval volumes of the *History of the King's Works*, but even though the castle was occasionally in royal hands, Tattershall is not accorded a discrete entry.[12] We should also note that a second scholar, E.M. Myatt-Price, was working on an edition of the Tattershall accounts for 1475–6 (also amongst the Penshurst Manuscripts) whilst Simpson was working on his *LRS* edition.[13] There is no reference to Myatt-Price's work in Simpson's volume (nor, it must be said, *vice-versa*) and Simpson only extracted a short fragment for publication from these household accounts, concerning building works on the estate in 1472. The 1475–6 accounts deal almost exclusively with provisions for the castle and contain little material relevant to the fabric itself. A valuable study of Ralph Cromwell's wills was published in 1990.[14]

shire', *Country Life* 190/41 (1996), 50–55; J. Musson, 'To me the past is sacred …', *Country Life* 192/2 (1998), 34–37.

6 O. Creighton, *Castles and Landscapes* (London, 2002); R Liddiard, *Castles in Context: Power Symbolism and Landscape, 1066–1500* (Macclesfield, 2005); A. Lowerre, *Placing Castles in the Conquest: Landscape, Lordship and Local Politics in the South-eastern Midlands, 1066–1100*, BAR (BS) 385 (Oxford, 2005); D. Austin, *Acts of Perception: A Study of Barnard Castle in Teesdale* (Newcastle, 2007); O. Creighton and R. Liddiard, 'Fighting Yesterday's Battle: Beyond War or Status in Castle Studies', *Medieval Archaeology* 52 (2008), 161–169.

7 P. Everson and D. Stocker, 'Masters of Kirkstead: Hunting for Salvation', *Kings Lynn and the Fens: Medieval Art, Architecture and Archaeology,*. BAA Conference Transactions XXXI (Leeds, 2008), 83–111; D. M. Wilson and D. G. Hurst, 'Medieval Britain in 1967', *Medieval Archaeology* 12 (1968), 168–9.

8 P. Everson and D. Stocker, 'The archaeology of vice-regality, Barlings, Kirkstead and Tattershall after the Lincolnshire Rising', in D. Gaimster and R. Gilchrist (eds), *The Archaeology of Reformation* (London, 2003), 145–58; P. Everson and D. Stocker, *Custodians of Continuity: The Premonstratensian Abbey at Barlings and its Landscape* (Heckington, 2010).

9 M. Gaimster and K. O'Connor, 'Medieval Britain and Ireland in 2004', *Medieval Archaeology* 49 (2005), 388.

10 J. Munby, J. Rhodes and Oxford Archaeology, 'Tattershall Castle, Lincolnshire: Conservation Plan' (National Trust internal document, 2009).

11 I. K. Bailiff, 'Methodological developments in the luminescence dating of brick from English late-medieval and post-medieval buildings', *Archaeometry* 49/4 (2007), 827–851.

12 R. A. Brown, H. M. Colvin and A. J. Taylor, *The History of the King's Works, Volume I: The Middle Ages,* ed. H. M. Colvin (London, 1963).

13 E. M. Myatt-Price, 'The Tattershall Household Book, 1475–76', *Lincolnshire Architectural and Archaeological Society Reports and Papers* 7/2 (1958), 126–56.

14 R. L. Friedrichs, 'The two last wills of Ralph, Lord Cromwell', *Nottingham Medieval Studies* 34 (1990), 93–112.

INTRODUCTION

I

LORD CROMWELL'S CASTLE

It may well be doubted whether in all the length and breadth of England there can be found a manorial *ensemble* of the later Middle Ages equal in fascinating interest to that which Ralph, third Baron Cromwell, created in the middle years of the fifteenth century at his Lincolnshire seat of Tattershall. Castle and pleasance, church, college, almshouse, school, market-stance, mill and village are here found, not as isolated and self-sufficient elements, but grouped together into an articulated whole, and carried out on an amplitude of scale and with an architectural splendour that has few parallels in the country.[1]

The evidence seems clear that the original manorial centre was not at Tattershall but about a mile to the north-east, at the village of Tattershall Thorpe, which is mentioned in Domesday, at the time of which survey (1086) it belonged to one of William's knights, Sir Eudo Fitzspirewic. No doubt the present castle of Tattershall took its origin from the licences to fortify and to crenellate granted by Henry III to Eudo's fourth descendant, Robert de Tateshale, in 1231 and 1239.[2] Of this earliest castle important remains were uncovered during the excavations conducted by the late Lord Curzon between 1912 and 1914, and other information can be gleaned both from documentary evidence and from the engraving published in 1726 by Samuel Buck. Conformably to the style of castle in vogue at its period, it consisted of a single stone-and-lime envelope with round flanking towers but apparently lacking a donjon. At the north-east corner was the gatehouse. Outside there was a single wet ditch, leaving the usual interval—known as *les lices* in mediæval parlance—between stone shell and water envelope.[3] Within the enclosure, against the west curtain, were stone domestic buildings —hall, solar, kitchen and chapel. Close east of the castle, probably more or less on the site of the present building, stood the parish church, apparently a Norman structure;[4] and the village no doubt

[1] See *Tattershall Castle*, by the Marquis Curzon and H. Avray Tipping (1929); also A. Hamilton Thompson, *Tattershall: the Manor, the Castle, the Church* (National Trust, ed. 1946).

[2] *Cal. Patent Rolls*, 1225–32, p. 435: Curzon and Tipping, p. 162.

[3] This is known because the magnesian limestone of the towers had not been in contact with the water—see Curzon and Tipping, *op. cit.* p. 163.

[4] *Op. cit.*, p. 3. Preserved in the Great Stable at the Castle are two Norman stones: (1) a nook cap, cushioned, with scallops and the half-cone moulding in the hollows; (2) a voussoir with chevroned enrichment. In the Castle Museum are two other Norman pieces: (1) a corbel with a grotesque human mask; (2) a large grotesque "beak-head".

long before Lord Cromwell's time had taken shape on the slightly rising ground to the north—for already in 1201, before the licence for the stone castle was granted, the father of its builder had obtained a gift of the right to hold a weekly market at Tattershall. The site is naturally a strong one, on a slightly rising ground, having the River Bain immediately to the east and the Witham about a mile to the west. These two streams unite a mile or more below Tattershall, which therefore stands in a kind of Y-shaped tongue of land between them, protected thus on three sides, and facing the not easily passable heath-lands and stanks that in the Middle Ages extended northward towards Horncastle and the Wolds.

In 1367 the manor of Tattershall came into the hands of Ralph, first Lord Cromwell, in right of his marriage to Maud Bernack, heiress of the line of Eudo. It was his grandson, Ralph, third baron, and Lord Treasurer of England from 1433 to 1443, who carried out on a sumptuous scale the re-fashioning of the whole manorial centre. He was a man of vast wealth and a magnificent builder, as appears not only by his works at Tattershall, but also by the stately residence which he erected for himself at his other property of Wingfield in Derbyshire.

The building accounts show that work upon the castle was actually in progress between 1434 and 1446. Cromwell's operations may be summarised as follows. He added a second moat round the castle, leaving a fairly narrow platform on the north, east and west sides,[1] but expanding southward so as to enclose a large tract of land in which was a pleasance, with fish-ponds on the opposite side of the moat. The narrow northern platform was divided by a cross-ditch so as to form two outer wards, both of which had to be traversed, by a devious approach over a series of well-defended bridges, before the innermost ward (the enclosure of the ancient castle) was reached. The early domestic buildings were in part reconstructed and in part replaced; and as thus reorganised they comprised a great hall, lying north and south, with a two-storeyed annexe at its north end, containing a parlour and an upper chamber. To the west side of these buildings, and connected with them by a corridor of access on the ground and first floors, Lord Cromwell added, as his own private residence, the colossal tower-house in brick, which alone of all these structures now remains, and is the glory of Tattershall—beyond any doubt, as Lord Curzon said, " the most splendid piece of brickwork in England ".[2] At the lower end of the hall, and in contact with it, were the kitchens, and the freestanding chapel[3] projected eastward into the courtyard. In the two outer wards

[1] The discovery of burials on the scarp of the eastern moat (where marked on plan, Fig. 1) suggests that Cromwell may have taken in a bit of the old churchyard here.

[2] *Op. cit.*, p. xiii.

[3] Dedicated to St. Nicholas, see *De L'Isle and Dudley MSS.*, vol. I, p. 171.

there were various buildings, including a wool-house and a large brick stable on the west side. Cromwell's household at Tattershall was on a lavish scale, for we are told that it consisted of at least a hundred persons.

Lord Cromwell also pulled down the old parish church and began to replace it by another of imposing dimensions and exquisite beauty. The new church, dedicated to the Holy Trinity, was endowed by its founder as a collegiate establishment, served by seven chantry priests or chaplains (including the warden), six secular clerks, and six choristers. In accordance with the common practice of the time, the nave was assigned for parochial uses and the choir apportioned to the college. Building accounts show that the work was still going on in 1482; the glass was not set in the windows until 1480 and 1481, while the architectural detail of the tower and of the *pulpitum*—the solid stone screen dividing the collegiate choir from the parochial nave—points to the very end of the fifteenth century, or even later. Cromwell died in 1456, and one of his executors was the famous William Waynflete, Bishop of Winchester, Lord Chancellor of England, and founder of Magdalen College, Oxford. Bishop Waynflete's arms appear over the north porch of the church. The college buildings, of which the merest scraps of foundations (encumbered by farm sheds) now remain, stood close east of the choir, and north of the nave was a row of bedehouses, with accommodation for thirteen beneficiaries. These bedehouses, which existed before Cromwell's time, were rebuilt in 1486, and included a lodging for the vicar of the parish. The present buildings do not seem to be older than the sixteenth century. If not before, at all events by Lord Cromwell's time, the village had assumed its present lay-out round the spacious market stance to the north of the church,[1] with a school on the east side[2] and the old market cross, which still shows the Lord Treasurer's arms, in the centre.[3] The castle moats were fed by an intake from the Bain, and this intake also served the manorial mill. To ensure a constant water-supply a stone weir was constructed just below the intake. The surplus water from the moats was carried back into the Bain by an outlet channel.

Such was the *ensemble* which the powerful Lord Treasurer created at his manor of Tattershall. In all respects it was thoroughly

[1] In 1449 nine shops are mentioned "on the north side of the market of Tateshale", *De L'Isle and Dudley MSS.*, vol. I, p. 226.

[2] Mr. Tipping (*op. cit.*, p. 107) says that "Cromwell's College was not educational, except in so far as its choristers needed tuition". But the statutes lay down that grammar is to be taught not only to the choristers but to "all sons of tenants of the Lordship of Tattershall and of the College without charge"—*De L'Isle and Dudley MSS.*, vol. I, p. 182. Probably therefore the College was the parent of the school. The ancient schoolhouse, in brick like that of the castle, with the four-centred arched doorways and other voids in Ancaster stone, still remains, though in poor condition.

[3] The cross on top is modern, substituting an urn which had replaced the original cross.

characteristic of its time. Professor Hamilton Thompson sums up the matter exceedingly well:[1]

"The establishment of such bodies of priests in the neighbourhood of their principal residences was a common habit of the great noblemen of the fourteenth and fifteenth centuries, just as their predecessors had founded monasteries, and Edward III's colleges of St. George at Windsor and St. Stephen at Westminster gave a lasting vogue to the practice. It is noteworthy that in 1434 the rebuilding of the church of Fotheringhay had been begun for the service of the college founded and maintained close to their castle by the Dukes of York, and that in 1440 Henry VI was engaged in the foundation of his college at Eton, close to Windsor Castle, and its sister college at Cambridge. Just so, Cromwell, while converting Tattershall Castle into a Windsor of his own, prepared to establish at its doors a corporation of clergymen, whose first duty should be to celebrate mass daily for the benefit of his soul and those of his relations and ancestors, and for other purposes indicated by him. In addition to this the foundation had its educational side, principally on account of the six choristers who formed part of it, and thirdly, the priests had to look after the almsmen and almswomen, thirteen in number,[2] whom Cromwell lodged in the building on the north side of the church. It should be realised that the warden and chaplains of Tattershall were not monks, but ordinary priests bound by no monastic rule; but it was intended that they should live together in one dwelling, similar to a college at Oxford or Cambridge, with a common hall, and with stipends derived from a common fund. . . . It is rarely that two great buildings, illustrating two distinct phases of the architecture of their age with great completeness, and each of them the product of a single design which has been maintained throughout their building, can be seen side by side. The juxtaposition of the great tower of Tattershall Castle and the collegiate church is in this respect unusually interesting. The tower is one of the few structures to which the misused epithet unique can be applied with real justice: nowhere in England is there anything quite like it. The church is less uncommon; but in a county famous for its fine churches it is, taken as a whole, the finest church of its period, and, in its splendid proportions and unity of conception, is not behind the best fifteenth century churches of East Anglia and Somerset. If the memory of the man to whom we owe them, a statesman and politican of an age when first-rate men of the type were

[1] *Tattershall Castle*, pp. 25, 29.

[2] Professor Thompson says "of each", but the deed of foundation makes it clear that the provision was for thirteen of either sex. *Cf.* also the contract for its rebuilding in 1486, in the *De L'Isle and Dudley MSS.*, vol. I, pp. 175–76.

> wanting in England, is somewhat dim, they yet remind us of the ambition and magnificence of a nobleman of the later Middle Ages, and of the religious observance which he regarded as a necessary part of his duty."

The mighty tower-house (see plans, Fig. 2 and views, Figs. 3 and 4) that Lord Cromwell added to the old castle of the de Tateshales is one of the most astounding architectural achievements that the Middle Ages have bequeathed to us in any country. It measures 62 feet by 48 feet over the walls, which in the basement are no less than 12 feet in thickness, while the total height, to the coping of the turret merlons, is fully 118 feet. The walls are built of red brick, made from the local Kimmeridge clay, in Old English bond; but the basal plinth, the various stringcourses, and the dressings of the voids are carried out in stone—in the plinth, of green or red Salmonby sandstone, which has well resisted the water of the moat, and above, of warm grey Ancaster limestone (from the lower Oolite), which, like the brickwork, has weathered excellently.[1] At all four corners of the tower are stout octagonal turrets, which rise above the main building and finish with crenellated parapets carried forward on brick corbels and pointed archlets. The main building, which is four storeys in height, above a basement below the courtyard level, has a heavy oversailing, machicolated parapet resting on enormous stone corbels of three filleted courses united by trefoiled archlets also in stone. Above this the wall-heads are organised in two stages. The lower, opening in a series of arches from the flat roof, has a row of square-headed and traceried windows to the field, and forms a covered way from which the *mâchicoulis* were served. The upper stage, or wall-walk proper, has a crenellated parapet. Above the wall-head rises, on the west side, a single short chimney, and, on the east side, a tall triple chimney stack (partly restored) of very ornate and elegant design.

Over the basal plinth, on the west front and two ends of the tower, where it rises out of the water, are two splayed offsets, the upper one of which is returned, at a slightly higher level, on the east or courtyard front. At the second floor level, a splayed stringcourse runs all round the tower; at the floor above, a similar stringcourse is found on the four turrets only. There are also moulded stringcourses below the battlements, both on the main building and on the turrets. All the battlements have stone copings, both on the merlons and on the embrasures; but these wall-head features have been much restored. The four turrets once had pyramidal leaded roofs. In the brick work, diaper patterns formed of "burnt ends" are spasmodically apparent. The contrast between the rich and broad, dark red brick wall surfaces and the greyish

[1] For this Ancaster stone, see *Victoria County History, Lincolnshire*, vol. II, p. 393.

green Ancaster stonework of the stringcourses, windows, and battlements is most effective.[1]

On the west side of the tower, in each of the four main storeys, are a pair of large, two-light windows, having a drop-centred, pointed arch under a hood mould. Each window consists of two pointed and cusped lights, with Perpendicular tracery in the head. On the south side there are three such windows, on the ground floor and on the first and third floors respectively, as well as a window, smaller, but still of two lights, which opens from the basement, and a similar window, of one light only, at the second floor level. On the north side we have a small basement window of two lights; large two-light windows on the ground and second floors; and smaller single-light windows on the other two floors. All these but one are of pointed form. On the east or courtyard side there are three pointed doors into the tower. Two in the main building lead down to the basement and in to the ground floor respectively; while the third door admits to the newel stair in the south-eastern turret. Between the two doors in the main building are two small windows, one above the other. Over the doors a couple of rows of large joist-holes and a roof-chase mark the position of the two-storeyed gallery which connected the tower-house with the hall, great chamber, and other buildings of the older castle. Above this again are three rows each of three windows, all but two of the usual form, pointed, with two lights; the two exceptions, both on the first floor, are square-headed, and one is of a single light only. The windows in the turrets are mostly of two lights: they are sometimes pointed and sometimes square-headed, and are arranged to suit the turret chambers, and, in the south-east turret, to light the stair. In this turret, at first floor level, a door communicated with the kitchen, which adjoined the tower-house on the south side. Above the wall-head of the main building, the turrets display crosslet loopholes, with oilettes at the extremities. Upon the two eastern turrets are the marks of the round towers of the thirteenth-century castle against which these turrets abutted: for which reason, this pair of turrets have little projection from the courtyard side of the castle, whereas the other pair are thrust boldly out into the moat.

The basement of the tower-house contains a dark store, spanned by a low segmental brick vault, with vaulted cells in three of the turrets; the staircase turret at this level is solid. In the floor is a well, now closed. At this level, the east wall of the tower attains a thickness of nearly 15 feet, and contains a vaulted chamber, possibly a prison. Although the walls decrease as the tower rises, this relative extra thickness of the east wall is maintained throughout

[1] The London and North Eastern Railway had a poster of Tattershall Castle by Fred Taylor, which brings out the colour values and the whole dramatic force of the great tower better than any other picture of it that I have seen.

its height, and the wall is hollowed out into a series of galleries and closets, which constitute one of the most remarkable peculiarities of this castle.[1]

The ground floor contains a large hall, lit by two windows on the west side and one in each end wall. The door on the east side has a vaulted guard-room adjoining. In the south-east corner is a garderobe, and in the three other turrets are lofty vaulted chambers. Midway in the east wall is the first of the three magnificent chimney-pieces—the finest of their kind in Britain—which are the glory of Tattershall, and the removal of which, in 1911, prior to their export across the Atlantic, was the immediate cause of the purchase of the Castle by the late Lord Curzon, his dramatic recovery of the fireplaces, his restoration of the tower-house and other remains, and his noble bequest of the property to the nation.

There is no communication between this ground floor room and the upper storeys, which are reached by the newel stair in the south-east turret. This stair, which comprises 149 steps, is a truly monumental piece of construction. The steps are of stone, and their canted under surfaces form a continuous winding ceiling, ascending with the rise of the steps. A stone moulded hand-rail is sunk in the staircase wall. On the first floor is the great hall, also with a splendid chimney-piece, in the east wall towards the north end, where the dais was, as shown by the corbels which carried the wall plate of a tester over the " high board ". This hall has two large windows on the west side and one in the south wall. It is entered from the stair by a lobby, with an octopartite groined vault, and beyond this lobby, in the thick eastern wall, is a long narrow, corridor-like, vaulted chamber. Large vaulted closets occupy the three turrets, and from the north-western of this opens a vaulted garderobe in the north main wall. The western windows have groined and ribbed vaults, while the southern window has a ribbed barrel-vault. The use of this hall as the lord's private dining room is testified by the door (now blocked) which communicates, across the newel stair, with the kitchen.

The second floor room formed the *camera* or great chamber. It is entered from the staircase by means of a lofty corridor extending the whole length of the east wall. The corridor has five bays of quadripartite ribbed vaulting, the stone bosses carrying heraldic shields; and it has been justly claimed for this passage that, " combining dignity of proportion with simplicity of detail ", it is " unexcelled by any other piece of brick architecture in England ".[2] At the far end of this passage are two doors, one admitting into the vaulted north-east turret chamber, which has a fireplace and a garderobe, while the other enters what was the lower end of the

[1] In Scotland, the fifteenth century Tower of Comlongan, Dumfriesshire, is designed in much the same way.

[2] Professor Hamilton Thompson in Curzon and Tipping, *op. cit.*, p. 177.

great chamber: for the plan is here reversed, as compared with that of the hall below—the upper end of the great chamber (with corbels for a tester) being towards the south, and its fireplace, the third of the famous series, being in the west wall, and the garderobe in the south wall. The purpose of this reversal of the plan is obvious and may be best set forth in the words of Mr. Avray Tipping:[1]

> "Here is all the apparatus for a great chamber of ceremony and audience. The suitors or visitors passed from the staircase into a narrow and beautifully vaulted gallery, lit by three double-light windows in the east wall. They had to travel the 40-feet length before reaching the doorway into the great chamber. If kept waiting they could enter the north-east turret room which was fitted with both a fireplace within it and garderobe through it. As each one's turn of admission came, he was thus ushered in at the passage end and thence approached the great man who stood, or sat, at the other end, backed by the rich hangings of a cloth of state."

The great chamber is lit by a window on either side of the fireplace, and by a third in the north wall. The north-east turret chamber has already been mentioned; the other two present no features of note.

The third floor of the tower-house formed the solar or lord's private room. It reverts, almost precisely, to the arrangements of the great hall. Though not quite so rich as the others, the fireplace is perhaps the most beautiful of the whole four. The staircase lobby has a quadripartite ribbed vault with sexpartite cusped ceiling in each compartment, and elaborate stone heraldic bosses. Two of the window bays have similar traceried vaulting—if the phrase may be admitted.

The newel stair, after giving access to the flat roof of the tower, terminates, and a smaller stair, winding up in the thickness of the turret wall, ascends to the wall-walk, behind the battlements and above the covered gallery from which the machicolations were served. This gallery opens directly from the flat roof through the series of arches already mentioned. Although in their present form these arches are a restoration, they follow the original design.[2]

In this splendid tower there are many minute and interesting details, illustrating the constructive ingenuity and artistic capacity devoted to its building, but these do not fall within the scope of the present enquiry.[3] For the same reason, I must resist the temptation to descant upon the sumptuous fireplaces, and so content myself, for the sake of completeness, with reproducing the

[1] *Op. cit.*, p. 78.

[2] See *A Topographical Account of Tattershall* [by George Weir], 3rd edition (1813), p. 6.

[3] The less so because the tower has been described with such amplitude and competence by Professor Thompson and Mr. Tipping.

short summary of their main characteristics given by Professor Hamilton Thompson:[1]

> "The general design of these is similar, a wide arched recess enclosed within a rectangular frame with the upper edge battlemented and with lateral shafts, while below the edge a succession of panels, each containing a shield or badge, is carried above the flat curve of the arch. In this the ordinary fashion of the day is followed; but the design is varied upon each floor with surprising freshness of imagination, and with a delicacy of carving which increases in minuteness with each stage. The succession of shields is different in each case, and the fireplace upon the second floor introduces panels carved with foliage in the place of heraldic emblems, while upon the ground floor the row of shields is doubled, and is broken by the upward curves of the ogee fire-arch. The shields are those of the various persons connected with Tattershall by ownership and family ties. . . . They are diversified, as has been said, by badges and other emblems, among which the purse, said to be emblematical of Cromwell's office of treasurer, is repeated again and again."

It has been pointed out[2] that the sprays of foliage shown on the fireplaces are a conventionalised portrayal of the Cromwell weed (*lithospermum officinale*)—evidently forming a rebus or punning allusion to the owner's name.

From the foregoing description it will be noted that this mighty tower contains, in general, the usual accommodation found in numerous other English and Scottish tower-houses of the fourteenth and fifteenth centuries: cellarage in the basement, the great hall on the first floor, the *camera* on the floor above, and the solar over all. But at Tattershall, between the cellarage and the hall, on the true ground floor, there is interpolated another apartment, the use of which is not so readily apparent. It has been described as a guard room "allotted to retainers".[3] But the magnificent fireplace forbids the assumption of any such subordinate purpose: moreover, as a guard room it would have been worse than useless, since the apartment has no communication with the stair and the room above. Retainers posted here could guard nothing, and would be of no service to anybody. Its isolation shows that this room served a purpose apart from the main life of the tower house; and, as we shall see, the whole theory of Cromwell's tower is that it was his own proper lodging, built to separate him from his retainers and to serve his particular purposes. None the less, this room with its grand chimney piece is an apartment of state like all the others

[1] *Tattershall: the Manor, the Castle, the Church*, p. 23.
[2] See *Antiquaries' Journal*, vol. VI, pp. 163–65.
[3] Thompson, *op. cit.*, p. 21; Curzon and Tipping, *op. cit.*, p. 75.

in the tower; and we can hardly be wrong in identifying it as a court of justice, like the corresponding room of the great tower-house in the archiepiscopal palace at Sens.[1] Here, we may be sure, Lord Cromwell, or his bailiff in his absence, would preside over the feudal courts of the barony of Tattershall.

The complete disappearance of all the other buildings has left Lord Cromwell's great tower standing stark and lonely. Its present isolated position, and the unusual size and splendour of its design, have always attracted deep interest and wonder; and many have been the speculations about its real purpose and as to the source from which Lord Cromwell derived the idea of so astonishing a structure. Most of these speculations have been coloured by fanciful analogies between the brick tower-house and the rectangular stone keeps which were in use during the Norman period. But long before Cromwell's time such keeps had ceased to be erected: the whole scheme of the thirteenth century castle into which he fitted his tower precludes a defensive keep of this sort. Such false analogies have obscured the fact that the tower is essentially a domestic structure, an integral part of a suite of residential buildings the rest of which have been stripped away from it.

Under this misconception, it has been usual to think of Lord Cromwell's tower-house as a conscious architectural atavism. Professor Hamilton Thompson, after remarking (very properly) that the group of small brick tower-houses in the eastern midlands are to be regarded as inspired by the great tower at Tattershall, and not as prototypes of it, concludes that "the tower is neither a following of contemporary fashion nor the glorification of a local type. It is a deliberate return to the donjon of earlier days, but in adaptation the donjon, a structure designed for defensive warfare, is transformed into a habitable and splendid dwelling". And again: "Its scale is that of the rectangular castle keeps of the twelfth century, and it is with them that it may most fitly be compared".[2]

As a matter of fact, the Tattershall tower-house, so far from being a "deliberate return" to an obsolete idea, is in the very forefront of "contemporary fashion" in the secular architecture of western Europe. A right understanding of its affinities adds enormously to the interest of this most remarkable structure.

The primary principle of the dwelling-house in Northern Europe was the great hall used for all purposes, one large compartment under a single span of roof—contrasting fundamentally with the Mediterranean plan of a house composed of many apartments serving different ends, as seen, for example, in a Roman "villa". Such a hall, in addition to providing for the needs of family life,

[1] See Viollet-le-Duc, *Dictionnaire d'Architecture,* vol. VII, p. 479.
[2] Curzon and Tipping, *op. cit.*, p. 182; Thompson, *op. cit.*, p. 12.

with its great length and lofty roof formed an outward and visible sign of the importance of the owner. Under the feudal system it served also for various public purposes, such as the holding of baronial courts or the management of estate business. "It played a part in the public life of a self-contained community which can hardly be realised in our own day, supplying its chief means of contact with the life of the world outside. Just as the hall of the royal palace at Westminster became the centre of English national life, so on a smaller scale the manorial hall was of similar importance to the district which depended on its lord ".[1]

The mediæval word for a house on the hall-plan was *palatium*; and it was so translated in Scotland, where a "palace" or a "house built palace-wise", has this strict special sense.[2] I propose, therefore, in the following discussion to speak of the "palatial" plan, using the term in its proper mediæval significance.[3]

This conception of a great hall persisted as the nucleus of the domestic buildings in the stone castles of the later Middle Ages; but it came to be modified in two ways, and at both ends. At the upper, or "dais" end, private or "solar" apartments were added for the lord and his family. At the lower or "screens" end, a separate kitchen, with pantry and buttery accommodation, superseded the primitive practice of cooking in the open court, or at a central hearth in the hall. Such a composite structure forms the normal dwelling house of the later Middle Ages in England, whether free-standing, as at Aydon Hall, or enclosed within a towered wall of *enceinte*, as was the case of Tattershall Castle itself before it was re-handled by Lord Cromwell.[4] In France during the last two centuries of the Middle Ages, this palatial plan underwent much further development. The introduction of groined vaulting led to the strengthening of the sides of the buttresses and the casing of the angles by square or circular clasping projections, often capped by or rising into turrets. The architectonic need for these consolidations impeded the growing desire for spacious windows to light the hall, hence a tendency to concentrate these openings in one wall, usually a narrow one; and from this tendency, again, with the increasing sense of the decorative value of large traceried windows in the later phases of Gothic art, came the development of one side of the building as a "show-front". At the same time, the growing power of the means of attack led to the heightening of

[1] A. Hamilton Thompson, *The English House*, (Hist. Assoc. Pamphlet No. 105), p. 4.

[2] See W. Mackay Mackenzie, *The Mediæval Castle in Scotland*, cap. v.

[3] The standard work on the whole subject of the development of the "palatial" plan is Karl M. Swoboda, *Römische und Romanische Paläste*, 2nd ed., Vienna, 1924.

[4] We already find this tacking of specialised apartments on to the common hall in the Bishop of Durham's hunting lodge, *circa* 1183. It consisted of an aisled timber hall, 60 feet long and 16 feet broad between the posts, to which were attached a buttery, a steward's room, a *camera*, a garderobe, and a chapel, all enclosed by a palisade. See the Boldon Book in *Domesday Book*, vol. IV, p. 575; G. Baldwin Brown, *The Arts in Early England*, ed. 1926, vol. I, p. 104.

the building and to crowning it with an oversailing defensive parapet. With this added height the interior is divided into several storeys, forming a series of great halls, one above the other, each devoted to a special purpose.

As a result of all the processes the "palatial" plan in France tended in the fourteenth century to develope into a composite structure of great height, oblong on plan, with towers or turrets at the four corners and covered by a heavy machicolated parapet. Such a building assumed much of the external characters of the older donjons or defensive towers, but none the less it stands upon quite a different line of development. The older donjon was a complete structure in itself, forming the kernel of the castle, to which the other buildings were merely appendages or outworks. These new tower-houses, by contrast, were only part of a whole articulated building, serving in it the special purpose of the lord's private residence. Their isolation is not intended, as was the isolation of the older donjons, to enable them to hold out even after the rest of the castle had been taken: it is mainly designed to secure the privacy of the lord and his family. These fourteenth and fifteenth century tower-houses are in fact only a specialised type of solar, and are always associated with separate halls provided for the general household. The tower-house at Tattershall was linked up with such other accommodation; and its four doors of access—three from the main corridor and one from the kitchen—none of which are defended in any special way, reveal how remote it really is from the older donjon theme.

There can be little doubt that the development of this special type of castle was accelerated by the great change which was coming over the military art in the fourteenth century. Warfare was now becoming a higly specialised and scientific thing, in which the old tumultuary feudal levies, bound only to serve for short periods in a time, were of little use. More and more, therefore, the kings in their national quarrels, and the great barons in their incessant private feuds with each other, came to rely on mercenary soldiers whom they retained in their pay. Whereas in former days the castle, during times of peace, would contain only the lord's *familia* or household, it must now provide standing accommodation for a compact body of mercenary troops. The neighbourhood of these hard-boiled *Lanzknechts* would always be inconvenient and often dangerous, as they did not owe the natural allegiance of vassals, and were at all times liable to be tampered with by their employer's enemies. Hence, for reasons both of privacy and safety, the great lords of the fourteenth and fifteenth centuries took care to provide their castles with self-contained residences for their families and personal retainers.[1]

[1] For all this, reference may be made to my paper on "Bastard Feudalism and the later Castles" in *Antiquaries' Journal*, vol. XXVI, pp. 145–71.

Thus at the Château de Pierrefonds, erected about 1400, the great composite mass of building known as the donjon is really nothing more than a stately private residence for the lord of the castle, emphasising his exalted magnificence, securing him from intrusion, and providing for himself and his family ample and luxurious accommodation. It is not in any sense what the older donjons were, "the last stronghold of the fortress". Alongside it are ample halls for the general use of the establishment; these are on a sumptuous scale, but the dignity and pride of the lord are flaunted in the towering height and splendour of his own residence.[1]

The donjon of the *Palais de Justice* at Poitiers, built by the Duc de Berry between 1382 and 1388, is an oblong building, with a round tower at each corner (Figs. 5 and 6). It is now reduced to a couple of storeys, but originally it was carried up to a great height, and was crowned with a boldly oversailing machicolated parapet. The large and decorative windows are concentrated on one side, which thus forms a "show-front". The interior was divided into three stages, each of which contained a single lofty hall. Outwardly the building displays much of the martial aspect of the older donjon towers, but its real pedigree, as Viollet le Duc long ago saw, must be sought in another quarter:

> "*Le donjon du palais de Poitiers est à lui seul un petit château, possédant une grand'salle à chaque étage et des chambres dans les tours. Il affecte une apparence de forteresse, mais il n'est réellement qu'un gros logis éclairé par des larges baies et n'était nullement propre à la défense; il se rapproche de l'architecture civile, et les tours, les màchicoulis, ne sont la qu'un appareil féodal.*"[2]

Word for word and in every detail this description will apply to Lord Cromwell's tower-house at Tattershall. The identity of idea between the two buildings is patent. Note also that at Poitiers, as at Tattershall, the tower-house is in contact with a large hall which serves the general purposes of the household. Mr. Lucien Magne, in his book on this great donjon at Poitiers, has the following remark:[3]

> "*Chaque palais construit par le duc de Berry, à Bourges, à Poitiers ou à Riom, compris, comme le palais du roi, outre la grande salle, la tour féodale, le logis du duc et la sainte-chapelle.*"

If we equate the collegiate church with the *sainte-chapelle*,[4] there are just the constituent elements in Lord Cromwell's reorganisation of Tattershall.

[1] Sir Theodore Cook, *Twenty-five Great Houses of France*, p. xx.

[2] *Dictionnaire d'Architecture*, vol. VII, p. 10.

[3] *Le Palais de Justice du Poitiers*, p. 5.

[4] There is some evidence that Lord Cromwell reconstructed the existing castle chapel at Tattershall before founding the collegiate church. See Curzon and Tipping, pp. 172–73.

The same broad characteristics are shown in the tower-houses of the Château de Vincennes and the Château de Vez,[1] castles of about the same period as the Palais de Poitiers.

From France this "palatial" type of building spread to the west and east. Westward it reached England in 1433 at Tattershall, and at Holyrood appears in Scotland in the next century (Fig. 7). Eastward it provided one of the most notable monuments of the Middle Ages in the *Westbau* or great western extension made between 1380 and 1398 to the castle of the Grand Masters of the Teutonic Order at Marienburg in Prussia (Fig 8). Here we have the same association of a lofty tower-like structure, containing private accommodation, with an earlier hall. The two are linked together with a corridor of access similar in principle to that at Tattershall. Externally, the *Westbau,* with its ponderous angle buttresses recalling the turrets at Tattershall, its strongly developed *Schaufassade* or "show-front", and its great oversailing machicolated coronet, put there as much for effect as for military use, has affinities with the Lincolnshire tower that clearly establish their common pedigree. The *Westbau* at Marienburg was built by the great architect Klaus Fellenstein, who came from Koblenz, and Dr. Karl Heinz Clasen has demonstrated how the inspiration was derived from France.[2]

Thus we see that our tower-house at Tattershall, so far from being a revival of an obsolete form, was quite the most up-to-date thing Lond Cromwell could have built. The simplest assumption is that he borrowed the idea from the contemporary castles of France, in which he had done much military service: and the *provenance* of his tower is so far indicated in its covered in and machicolated wall-head gallery, which is common in French castles of the period, but is otherwise unknown in Britain.[3] In particular, the way in which the *mâchicoulis* are spanned by archlets uniting the corbels is in its origin a French mannerism. It is found also at Bodiam, Caister, Cooling, Hever, Hurstmonceaux, Leeds, Raglan and Scotney, and in the barbican of Lewes—all like Tattershall built more or less from the "spoil of the Gaul"; and on the south-east tower of Bothwell Castle in Scotland, erected probably by Archibald, fourth Earl of Douglas and Duke of Touraine.[4] Later, the fashion became domesticated in England, and is found, mostly on a toy scale, in many buildings of the Tudor period.

[1] Viollet-le-duc, *op. cit.*, vol. V, p. 94, over-emphasises the military side of this tower-house. The large fireplaces, the wide windows with their stone side-benches, and the ample garderobes, sufficiently mark the essentially residential character.

[2] *Der Hochmeister-palast der Marienburg*, chap. iii.

[3] On the other hand, the French preference was for a high pitched roof enclosing the gallery. This is found also in the *Deutschordensburgen*. At Tattershall the flat roof, necessitating an upper wall-walk with open battlements, may be thought of as an English modification.

[4] See my paper in *Trans. Glasgow Archæol. Soc.*, n.s., vol. XI, pp. 97–116; also the *Official Guide* (Ministry of Works).

The rectangular donjons of Norman and Angevin times had fallen out of favour by the beginning of the thirteenth century. Except in what I have elsewhere described as the "northern tower-house province",[1] no more of them were built in England after that time. With such earlier towers, Tattershall has little in common: from them, it is parted by more than two centuries of broken tradition. Its real affinities and pedigree must be sought overseas. I cannot feel that Professor Hamilton Thompson is justified in claiming that in Lord Cromwell's tower "the military architecture of an earlier period was studied with great intelligence, and some of its features were ingeniously adapted".[2]

On the contrary, the internal plan and domestic accommodation of the tower embody the requirements of its age, and are far in advance of what is found in any Norman keep: while its military or quasi-military features are simply those of a contemporary French castle, and as such represent an architecture not so much of defence as of ostentation. Lord Cromwell was an up-to-date man in every way, and there was no need for him to study the military architecture of an earlier kind, however intelligently. He built to suit his own requirements, and in the most modern manner of his time. Conscious antiquarianism in design was never a failing of the Middle Ages, and at no time less so than in the fifteenth century. I am certain that any such motive was the very last thing present in the Lord Treasurer's thoughts.

Having thus cleared the ground of misconceptions, let us now look more closely into the question: whence did Lord Cromwell derive the design of his great brick tower? That the idea of it was French in its origin, and that some of its detail has a French aspect, we have already observed. Cromwell had campaigned in France, and it is easy to assume that he may have brought back with him the desire to build such a great residential addition to the old castle of the de Tateshales. On the other hand we should not exclude the possibility of the idea having come from further afield—not directly from France itself, but perhaps from some one of the regions into which, as we have found, the French invention of the "palatial" tower with its "show-front" had permeated. Unfortunately, the building accounts of Lord Cromwell's work nowhere reveal to us any one distinctly designated as the master mason. But we do learn the name of the man who made the bricks: and the choice of this material is itself perhaps significant: for, as Mr. Avray Tipping has shown, brick was a very rare material for castellated edifices in France until well after the time when Lord Cromwell's tower was built.[3] Now this brickmaker's name was *Bawdwin Docheman*, Baldwin the Dutchman. It has been

[1] *Archæologia Cambrensis*, 1942, p. 131.
[2] *Tattershall*, p. 12.
[3] Curzon and Tipping, *op. cit.*, pp. 56–58.

usual to say that he must have come from Flanders, and this conjecture derives some support from the known fact that Flemings were employed in various brick building operations in the eastern and south-eastern shires about this time. On the other hand, in the fifteenth century, and for long thereafter, the word Dutchman had not yet acquired its modern restricted significance: it then meant *Deutsch*, and may signify anybody of Teutonic origin, so that Baldwin may have come from anywhere within the German area. In Lord Cromwell's time the Hanseatic merchants in London were regularly known as Dutchmen:[1] and it would be easy to compile a long list of instances, from the fifteenth and sixteenth centuries, of the word Dutch in the sense of the modern German.[2]

In examining Tattershall I have been greatly struck with the resemblance of much of its detail to that found in the splendid brick castles of the Teutonic Order in Old Prussia. The quirked casement, or *Hohlkehle* as the Germans call it, is one of the most distinctive mouldings in the lands beyond the Vistula; and it is found repeatedly at Tattershall, for example, in the long gallery and in the heraldic vestibule on the third floor. The whole style of this gallery reminds me most forcibly of the East Prussian buildings. Also the way in which the monotonous red surfaces of the outer wall are broken up here and there by diapering in lozenge-shaped patterns of "burnt ends" is a trick regularly found throughout the Baltic area from the fourteenth century onwards. The military, diplomatic and commercial connexions between England and the Hanseatic league and the Teutonic Order in the fourteenth and fifteenth centuries are well known,[3] and the influence exerted by English architecture upon that of the Order has long been recognised by German students. We must therefore be on the lookout for evidences of an influence in the reverse direction, and should no longer adhere to the view that France and the Low Countries were the only sources of foreign influence upon English architecture in the later Middle Ages. Such evidences are in fact not far to seek. Thus, as has been elsewhere shown,[4] the remarkable brick castle, built by Sir John Fastolf at Caister, near Yarmouth—a great centre of the Hanse in England—is a perfect specimen of a Rhenish *Wasserburg;* and the connexions between England and the Rhineland, in the third Edward's reign and subsequently, are

[1] See J. H. Wylie, *Henry IV*, vol. II, p. 72.

[2] For example, take the following passage from Bishop Coverdale's *Prologue to the New Testament* (1535): "And to help me herein I have had sundry translations, not only in Latin, but also of the Dutch interpreters, whom, because of their simpler gifts and special diligence in the Bible, I have been the more glad to follow." Here the Bishop is manifestly speaking of the German reformers.

[3] See Dr. Bruno Schumacher, "*Der Deutsche Orden und England*" in *Altpreussische Beiträge, Festschrift zur Hauptversammlung des Gesamtvereins der deutschen Geschichts- und Altertumsvereine zu Königsberg,* 1933, pp. 5–33.

[4] *Antiquaries' Journal*, vol. XXXII, pp. 35–51.

familiar to all historians. (Sir John Fastolf, it is worth remembering, was a close friend of Lord Cromwell.) And if some of the brick-masons settled in England during the fifteenth century were Flemings, others certainly came from Germany. For example, at Ipswich in 1436 there dwelt Henry Herryson, "brikemaker, born in Teutonic parts"; and in Essex at West Horndon, in the same year, there was Henry Mason, born at Waltripp in Westphalia.[1] So also we have the three Bury St. Edmunds "brekebrennerys" who in 1430 are styled "*Teutonic*".[2]

Across the county from Tattershall, at Thornton Abbey on the shores of the Humber, Lincolnshire can show, in Abbot Thomas de Grettam's gatehouse, licensed in 1382, another great brick building, half a century older than Lord Cromwell's tower. Mr. Arthur Oswald has pointed out that the first floor plan of this gatehouse, "with its great hall surrounded by galleries, has a close resemblance to those of Tattershall Castle; but we do not here find that skilful use of cut and moulded brick which enabled the Tattershall builders to introduce elaborate brick vaulting into passages and guard-chambers".[3] While it is certain that the designer of Lord Cromwell's tower had closely studied the Thornton gatehouse, it is just in this "skilful use of cut and moulded brick" that I seem to detect an extraneous influence, in which I suspect connexions with the Hanseatic league and perhaps with the Teutonic Order.

We may take it for granted that Lord Cromwell would himself exercise a dominant control over the design of his tower-house. As Professor Hamilton Thompson remarks:[4]

> "It cannot, of course, be doubted that the design follows Lord Cromwell's wishes, and that he had considerable influence upon the plan. In the days before the profession of architect had become distinct from that of builder, the employer may well have had more control over the planning of his house than the modern architect allows him. His agent, as clerk of the works, was always on the spot to look after operations; and the fragmentary building accounts of Tattershall give us the names of three such agents, Thomas Croxby in 1434–5, John Southell in 1445–6, and John Combe in 1451–2. But the clerk of the works was not the architect. In such cases, the design was for practical purposes entrusted to men whose profession was building . . . and, apart from a few general ideas, the architect of the tower at Tattershall was, as in other places, the master-mason. He himself, and the freestone masons who worked under him would be responsible for the

1 *Cal. Patent Rolls*, 1429–36, pp. 566, 587.
2 L. F. Salzmann, *Building in England*, pp. 142, 589–90.
3 H. A. Tipping, *English Homes*, Periods I and II, vol. ii, p. 278.
4 *Tattershall*, pp. 19–20.

carved work of the fireplaces and windows; the bricklayers who did most of the work were under his supervision and subject to his control; and the master carpenter would work in conjunction with him. This is no imaginary picture, for it is the uniform procedure which can be derived from the study of mediæval building accounts."

While it is true that the Tattershall building accounts are fragmentary, for the years for which we have them they are complete enough to make it certain that, if there had been a master-mason additional to the brickmasons, rough masons, and freestone masons whose names we have, his name also would have been entered in the pay roll. Among the masons whose names we do have, Baldwin Dutchman—brickmason and brickmaker, as he is variously called—emerges as the most important and highest paid among the operatives, and as the only one in a position of authority. We find him making the bricks on an enormous scale at Edlington Moor, some few miles north of Tattershall, where the pits from which he dug his clay still remain. How vast were his operations there we may gather from the fact that in 1445–6 384,000 large bricks and 84,000 smaller ones had been prepared, not to speak of 274,000 bricks left over from the previous year. On the works of the great tower called "le Dongeon", and the works of the castle, 322,000 large bricks had been employed, and for the new "contremur" or revetment wall of "le Syncarr"—a pond as we learn from another entry—94,000 had been used, while 2,000 more had gone into John Warner's house in Tattershall and 5,000 into Edlington Church. As we have seen, the distinctive feature of Lord Cromwell's tower is the extensive use of shaped and moulded bricks, accurately adjusted to their positions in the fabric. All this moulding and shaping could have been done only in the closest dependence on the general design of the great tower. Having regard to all the circumstances, I have little doubt that Baldwin Dutchman, "brickmaker" and "brickmason" as he is indifferently called in the accounts, was in fact the master-mason or builder of the tower-house.

Professor Hamilton Thompson has provided us with a continental parallel, pointing out that "the master mason of Caudebec, who died in 1484, was Guillaume le Tellier, i.e. William Tyler".[1] Nor need we go so far afield. In England itself, Baldwin Dutchman's contemporary, William Veysey, was certainly employed both as a brickmaker and as that we should nowadays call an architect. On 10th October, 1434, William Veysey, "brikemaker, King's serjeant", "in order to speed the work on the King's manors at Shene and elsewhere", is instructed to search for earth suitable for making the tiles called "brike", and also to provide carriage for the same and the requisite labourers, iron, timber, roofing tiles,

[1] *Tattershall*, p. 20, footnote.

lead, stone, laths, lime, coal, firewood and other necessaries for making such "brike" and carrying on the said work.[1] This instruction was renewed to him on 12th January, 1445.[2] And on 4th July, 1442, William Veysey, "brikemaker", is appointed to take masons and layers (*positores*) called "brike leggers" for the works of Eton College at the King's wages, and to commit to prison all contrary therein.[3] From these entries it is as clear as crystal that Veysey was in executive charge of both undertakings.

Baldwin Dutchman was a man of enterprise. At Edlington he ran his own farm, for the accounts for the year 1445-6 record the sale to him of sheep and stock to the value of £2 9s. 4d. The Privy Council Register for the year 1437 contains a permission to one Baudwyn to import forty sarpliers (measures of wool) without custom.[4] This may be our Baldwin. It is worth nothing that his contemporary William Veysey was likewise interested in wool. In 1445 he had a grant for life of the wages of 6d. a day from the farm of the subsidy and ulnage on woollen cloths for sale in London and the suburbs thereof, and from a moiety of the forfeiture of the same, and of £10 yearly besides from the same.[5] Along with Richard Lounde he also had for life the search and correction of beer and beer-brewers;[6] and in 1451—now an esquire—he was associated with Richard Ady, mason, both of London, in a grant of the keeping of the demesne lands of the King's manor of Kenyngton, in Surrey. It is clear that master-brickmasons such as William Veysey and Baldwin Dutchman were men of standing and substance. Veysey in fact finished up as a member of Parliament.[7] Our Baldwin Dutchman was dead by 1457–58, but the brickmaking business was carried on by his widow, who in that year was paid £11 13s. 4d. for making 160,000 bricks.[8]

In Baldwin Dutchman—Baldwin the German as I hold him to have been—we must therefore salute, if my reading of the evidence be correct, the architect of one of the greatest English secular monuments of the Middle Ages.

II. THE BUILDING ACCOUNTS

The building accounts of Tattershall Castle which follow are preserved in the manuscripts belonging to Lord De L'Isle and Dudley at Penshurst Place. Along with a mass of documents

[1] *Cal. Patent Rolls*, 1436–41, p. 145. [2] *Op. cit.*, 1441–6, p. 365. [3] *Ibid.*, p. 93.

[4] *Acts of the Privy Council*, vol. V, p. 44.

[5] *Cal. Patent Rolls*, 1441–46, p. 365; *Cal. Close Rolls*, Henry VI, vol. IV, p. 260.

[6] *Cal. Patent Rolls*, 1436–41, p. 495; 1441–46, p. 365.

[7] See J. H. Harvey, *English Mediæval Architects*, p. 274.

[8] "*Et in denariis solutis uxori Baudwini Docheman pro factura et anulacione de clx.Ml tegularum capienti pro ml sic factis et anulatis xxijd ex veteri convencione per Dominum xiiij li. xiijs iiijd De quibus perdonantur communicacione et locucione magistri Gardiani cum dicta uxore ad opus Colleggii per ipsum concessa lx s et sic ultra:* xjli xiijs iiijd—*De L'Isle and Dudley Papers*, no. 219.

dealing with the Collegiate Church of Tattershall, they came into the muniment room at Penshurst through the fact that Sir Henry Sidney obtained the estates of the dissolved college as part of his share in the inheritance of Henry VIII's favourite Charles Brandon, Duke of Suffolk, to whom his doting master had granted the castle and manor of Tattershall and the collegiate church with its almshouses. The existence of the building accounts remained unsuspected until the Penshurst manuscripts came to be examined by the Historical Manuscripts Commission. An excellent short summary of their contents is printed at pp. 213–15 in Vol. I of their *Report on the Manuscripts of Lord De L'Isle and Dudley*, published in 1925. This summary was used by Mr. H. Avray Tipping when writing his book on Tattershall Castle, but he did not consult the originals.

The transcript upon which the present edition is based was made for me by Miss Lucy Drucker in the offices of the Historical Manuscripts Commission in London in 1943, *inter arma et bombos*. Cordial permission was given by the late Lord De L'Isle and Dudley, and every facility was courteously provided by the Commission's staff. Miss Drucker's transcript is an exact one, reproducing all the abbreviations and contractions of the original. For the extension of these in the printed text, and for the translation, I alone am responsible. Those familiar with medieval manuscripts are aware of the uncertainty that often lurks in the expansion of contracted words, particularly personal or place names. Where any serious doubt exists, an indication is always given. It should be added that in some cases the record is damaged by mutilation or damp.

In my translation and commentary, I have tried to follow the pattern set by Professor Hamilton Thompson in his admirable edition of the building accounts of Kirby Muxloe Castle. Thus in the earlier part of the translation I have given what is practically a *verbatim* English rendering of the Latin original: but the later portions have been somewhat condensed by the omission of purely formal repetitive phrases and mere words of style.

It must be emphasised that these building accounts have come down to us in a fragmentary condition. Unlike those of Kirby Muxloe, they do not tell the whole story. It is thus impossible to reconstruct the entire ordaining, devising and weekly progress of the undertaking, even to the alternate rhythm of summer and winter work, as has been done so brilliantly for Kirby Muxloe by Professor Thompson and the late Sir Charles Peers, and for Eton College by Professor Douglas Knoop and Mr. G. P. Jones. None the less, our Tattershall accounts are of high interest as the building record of one of the most important secular monuments of the later Middle Ages in Western Europe. They cast much light on the history of the fabric and the sources of its materials, and upon the way in which such an enterprise was conducted in England in the fifteenth century.

Scattered through the Tattershall papers at Penshurst are occasional minor records of building work at the castle. One such on a larger scale, accounting for repairs done in 1471–72, is included in the present volume.

The Kirby Muxloe accounts present us with a weekly record of all outlays connected with the work of building, so that we can follow the whole progress of the undertaking from start to finish. The Tattershall papers, on the other hand, give us not a current but a classified account. Each yearly statement begins with a note of arrears of payment from last year, these accounts having been submitted too late for inclusion in last year's returns. Then follows a detail of the whole moneys that came into the Clerk of Works' hands during the year, by imprests from Lord Cromwell's Receiver-General and his receivers in the several counties where he owned manors; by direct grants " from my lord's coffers ", and by sales of surplus stocks of timber, brick, faggots, and other materials; as well as any cash held as surpluses from the preceding year. Then follow the building costs of the Castle: purchase and carriage of stone, wages of stone masons, purchase or making of bricks, wages of brick masons, carpenters and joiners, labourers' wages, purchases of iron, lead, glass, quicklime, plaster of Paris, and other materials of every kind, and all sorts of travelling and miscellaneous expenses. The sources of the building materials are of much interest. Spanish iron is imported through Boston, ordinary iron is purchased and wrought at Coningsby and Tattershall. Wainscots—evidently " Eastland boards "—are imported through Hull. Freestone comes from Willesford and elsewhere. Bricks are made at Lord Cromwell's kilns at Edlington Moor and Boston. Building timber comes from Coningsby and Bardney, and some from houses taken down at Revesby Abbey. Glass of local manufacture is bought at Boston, plaster at Gainsborough and Granby. Coal comes from Boston, doubtless brought there by sea from Newcastle-upon-Tyne. The Accountant's salary is regularly entered, thought it was sometimes in arrears. Respites, or unpaid accounts, are duly listed, and the names noted of those to whom money is owing. The account concludes with an inventory of stock-piled materials—bricks, faggots, and so forth. It is to be assumed that what we have is the worked up, classified statement, prepared for the auditor, and based on a current or weekly expense account such as has been preserved in the case of Kirby Muxloe.

From the above summary it will be obvious that these accounts, imperfect though they are, present us with many items of much importance and interest. I have endeavoured to deal with these adequately in the Commentary which accompanies the English translation.

NOTES ON THE MANUSCRIPTS

I. Roll. no. 236 consists of five sheets of paper stitched head to foot making a roll 77¾ inches long and 11 inches wide. The head of the first sheet had been stitched to a piece of parchment of the same width which had acted as a protecting outer cover but which by its weight has now torn away part of the heading and the first two entries in a jagged piece. Though it is in need of repair it is mainly legible. It is possible that this roll is a draft and that the fair copy would have been made on parchment. There are many interlineations and cancellations which are shown in the printed roll in round brackets with " i " and " c " respectively beside them. It is noticeable that the parchment rolls surviving are well written and with few, if any, corrections.

II. Roll. no. 239 consists of two parchment membranes stitched together head to foot measuring 47 inches in all and about 11 inches wide. The whole of the right-hand side except for the last two inches is defective, having been torn irregularly. The left side is whole except for the last 6½ inches where a narrow piece has been torn away. It is written in a good clear hand, and appears to be a fair copy.

III. Roll. no. 246 (for the manor of Welby in Kesteven) is a single membrane of parchment 32 inches long by 11 inches wide. It is well written and appears to be a fair copy. Two entries only refer to Tattershall.

IV. Roll. no. 237 consists of two membranes of parchment stitched head to foot measuring 46 inches long by 11⅛ inches wide. It is slightly damaged on the right side. It is well written and appears to be a fair copy.

V. Roll. no. 239 is a single membrane of parchment 32 inches long by 11 inches wide. It is well written and appears to be a fair copy.

VI. Roll no 228 consists of eight paper sheets 11¼ inches wide. The fourth sheet only has been printed as the roll is a general one and not concerned solely with the buildings.

To face page xxxii

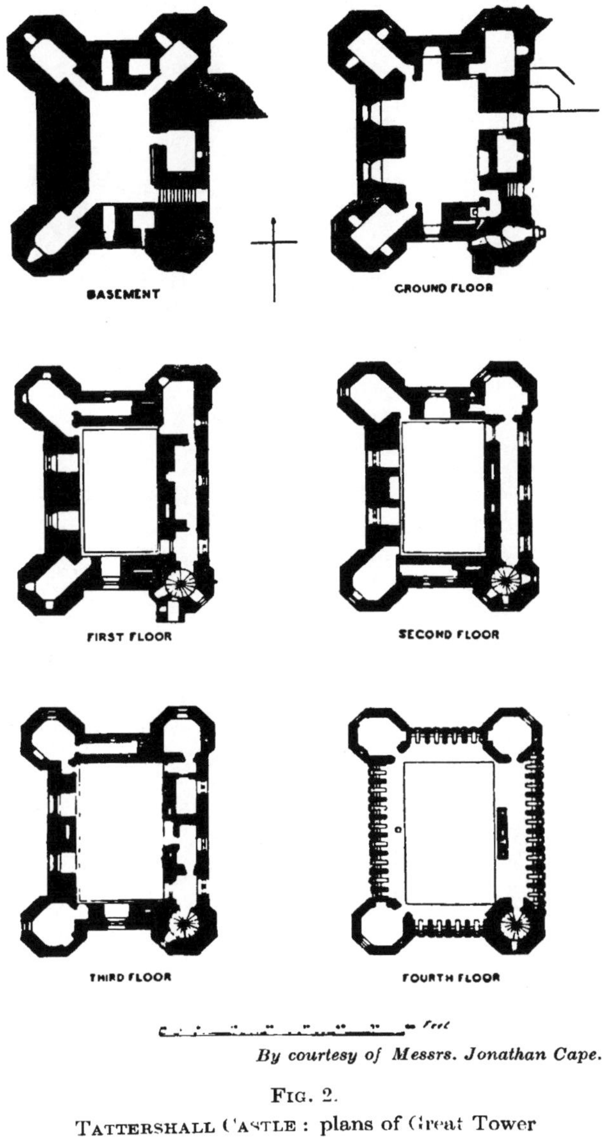

By courtesy of Messrs. Jonathan Cape.

FIG. 2.

TATTERSHALL CASTLE: plans of Great Tower

By courtesy of "Country Life".

FIG. 3.

TATTERSHALL CASTLE: Great Tower from west—the "show front".

By courtesy of "Country Life".

FIG. 4.

TATTERSHALL CASTLE: Great Tower from south, showing joist-holes for attachment of hall-gallery: foundations of kitchen buildings in moat in front and gable end of Great Stable behind tower on left side.

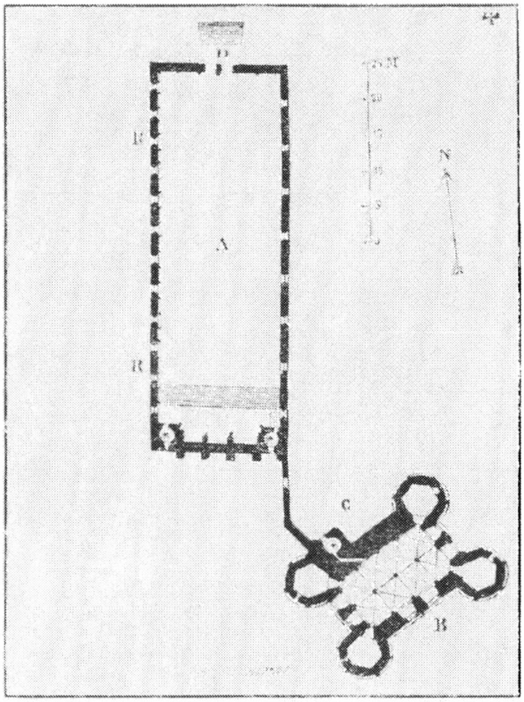

FIG. 5.
POITIERS: plan of Hall and Great Tower after Viollet-le-Duc.

FIG. 6.

POITIERS: elevation of Great Tower, the "show front", after Viollet-le-Duc.

FIG. 7.

THE PALACE OF HOLYROOD HOUSE from an engraving of 1650 showing combination of Hall with Great Tower having a "show front".

Fig. 8

Marienburg: The Grand Master's Palace. Hall to left; Great Tower in middle, with "show front". On the right is the *Hochschloss* (the conventual castle).

Tattershall Castle Building Accounts

I

15th February, 1434—2nd May, 1435

COMPOTUS THOME CROXBY OPERUM RADULPHI DOMINI CROMWELL CASTRI SUI DE TATESHALE SUPERVISORIS TAM [DE OMNIBUS ET] SINGULIS DENARIORUM SUMMIS PER IPSUM RECEPTIS QUAM DE SOLUCIONIBUS ET EXPENSIS PER IPSUM FACTIS A XV^{MO} DIE FEBRUARII ANNO REG[NI REGIS].... XIJ^{MO} USQUE IN SECUNDUM DIEM MAII ANNO EIUSDEM REGIS XIIJ^{MO} VIDELICET PER UNUM ANNUM INTEGRUM ET................DIE NEC ULTIMO COMPUTATO.

Arreragia (Marg.)

Nulla quia in superplusagio ultimi compoti.

Recepta denariorum de exitibus officii Receptoris Generalis (Marg.)

Set idem reddidit compotum de denariis receptis de exitibus officii Willelmi Stanlowe receptoris domini generalis per manus diversorum ministrorum denariorum soluencium super operibus castri predicti per tempus compoti prout tam in compoto ipsius receptoris generalis quam in compotis eorundem ministrorum (finiencium in festo sancti Michaelis anno xiij^{mo} predicto)[1] evidencius annotatur.

Et onerat se gratis. xlvij^{li} viij^{s} iij^{d}

Recepta denariorum de Gilberto Knaresburgh (Marg.)

Et de huiusmodi denariorum receptis de Gilberto Knaresburgh ut de parte recepte sue de coffro domini per tempus compoti prout per duas billas super compotum ostensas et inter huius compoti memoranda remanentes particulariter apparet quarum prima data xiiij^{mo} die Marcii anno xij^{mo} continet cxxxiij^{li} ix^{d} et secunda data primo die Maii anno xiij^{mo} continet lxxiiij^{li} iiij^{s} j^{d}. ccvij^{li} iiij^{s} x^{d}

Recepta denariorum de Roberto Gowshill clerico (Marg.)

Et de huiusmodi denariorum receptis de Roberto Gowshill clerico receptori domini in comitatibus Nottingham Derby et Leycester de exitu recepte sue ut de anno finiente in festo sancti Michaelis anno xiij^{mo} per ij billas indentatas remanentes ut supra quarum prima (data)^{c} incipiente xxv^{to} die Februarii anno xij^{mo} continet lxxix^{li} xvj^{s} xj^{d} et secunda incipiente xxx^{mo} die Januarii anno xiij^{mo} continet xij^{li} vj^{s} viij^{d} una cum centum solidis liberatis eidem computanti per ipsum receptorem sine billa. $\overset{xx}{iiij}$ xxxvij^{li} iij^{s} vij^{d}

Denarii recepti in precio iiij gaddorum ferri Ispannie (Marg.)

Et oneratur de precio iiij gaddorum ferri Ispannie de remanentia stauri domini anno precedente infra tempus compoti expenditorum super operibus castri predicti ponderantium $\overset{mi}{ccc}$xiiij libras precio singule centene v^{s} vj^{d} videlicet ut respondit ad precium huius ferri infra idem tempus empti apud Boston etc.[1] xvij^{s} ij^{d}

Denarii recepti in precio bosci et corticis de Stikeswold southwode et aliis boscis domini (Marg.)

Et oneratur (de)^{c} ut de precio $\overset{m}{xv}$ cxxiiij fagottorum (h)^{c} proveniencium de bosco et subbosco per tempus compoti succisorum in bosco domini vocatur Stikeswold Southwode super combustura tegularum (ad v thorale)^{c} apud torale domini tegulinum ibidem (precio singule millene xxxj^{s})^{c} (precio singule millene ultra facturam xxiij^{s} iiij^{d})[1] ultra $\overset{l}{M}$ $\overset{ma}{DC}$ $\overset{xx}{iiij}$ xvj fagottos assignatos priorisse de Stikeswold nomine decime etc.[1] xvij^{li} xij^{s} . . .

Et de precio corticis provenientis de bosco quercorum dicti bosci et subbosci venditi Roberto Fysshe in grosso (scilicet qualiter)^{c} quasi vj carecte precio singule carecte ij^{s}. xij^{s}

Et de precio lxxiiij carectarum focalii (h infra)^{c} (per)[1] tempus compoti prostrati infra chaceam de Tateshale pro x toralibus calcee vive comburendis super operibus predictis quasi ad quodlibet torale vij carecte

[1] *Sic.*

dimidia minus in toto dimidia carecta precio singule carecte secundum precium compoti precedentis xij^{d}. lxxiiij^{s}

Et de precio unius acre bosci et subbosci empte (de coffro domini)[1] (per tempus compoti)[c] de Abbate de Bardney (in bosco de Bardney)[1] mense Marcii anno xij^{mo} super operibus predictis (per est)[c] de cuius exitu et prostracione cxxx^{ma} quercubus provenerunt etc.[1] appreciat' per estimacionem secundum valorem aliarum acrarum contiguarum ad iiij^{li} vj^{s} viij^{d}

Et de precio ij acrarum dimidie huiusmodi bosci et subbosci emptarum de (Johanne Hert in (dicto)[c] bosco (abb')[c] dicti Abbatis de Bardney)[1] (eodem abbate mense)[c] et soluto de dicto domini coffro (proprio)[1] mense Marcii anno xiij^{mo} precio acre iiij^{li} vj^{s} viij^{d} una cum xv^{s} solutis dicto Johanni Hert de eisdem coffris domini ut pro prostracione dicti bosci videlicet acra ad vj^{s}. xj^{li} xi^{s} viij^{d}

Et de (ij^{s} x^{d})[c] precio xvij querculorum proveniencium de exitu copicie domini in chacea de Tateshale vocatur Thorpe Sheterley super operibus predictis precio singuli ij^{d}. ij^{s} x^{d}

Et onerat se gratis ut de precio DC^{ma} fagottorum (proven)[c] de parte M^{l}DC proveniencium de croppa et amputacione bosci predicte acre bosci empte de Abbate de Bardney ut superius (precio singule centene v^{s})[1] ultra M^{l} huiusmodi fagottorum cariatorum usque Tatershale super operibus predictis xxx^{s}

xxxix^{li} ix^{s} xj^{d} (Marg.)

Denariorum recepta in precio waynscott' emptorum apud Hull per dominum (Marg.)

Et oneratur se gratis de precio CC^{ma} tabularum vocatarum waynscott' proveniencium de providencia domini ex coffris suis propriis apud Hull et deinde mense Februarii anno xij^{mo} missarum usque Torkesey ac deinde usque Tateshale super operibus (etc.)[c] ibidem precio singule vij^{d}. vij^{li}

[1] *Sic.*

Denariorum recepta in precio mense operariorum in hospicio domini (Marg.)

Et oneratur ut de (precio)c denariis receptis de Johanne Crakehall' nuper custode hospicii domini in precio mense operariorum et laborariorum operancium super operibus castri predicti inter (xxiij)c xvm diem (Januarii)c Februarii anno xijmo et crastinum sancti Michaelis extunc proximum sequentem prout in compoto ipsius nuper custodis hospicii finiente in dicto (festo sancti)c crastino sancti Michaelis plenius apparet. xviijli iijs viijd

Respondit anno futuro (Marg.)

De precio mense huiusmodi operariorum operancium ibidem (et in eodem hospicio existencium)[1] inter dictum festum sancti Michaelis (anno et cla)c et ij diem Maii in clauso compoti non respondit (quia)c eo quod nondum factum (est)[1] scrutinium in libro (om)c dicti hospicii Ideo respondit anno futuro. nihil

Defalcaciones creditorum (Marg.)

Set onerat se gratis ut de denariis defalcatis super solucione facta Baldwino Brekeman' *xli* (tam)[1] pro factura tegularum vocatorum waltile propter insufficientiam (mixturam)[1] *ls vid* earundam tegularum (quam)c et denariis deductis pro cariago zabuli tam hoc anno quam anno precedente eo quod huiusmodi cariagium ex convencione supportabit etc.[1] quam pro denariis per ipsum relaxatis pro licencia habenda ad non intromittendum de *ls* deposicione (et)[1] removacione et culacione DCml tegularum hoc anno factarum post combustionem earundem videlicet singule Ml ad jd ex convencione facta per Johannem Fulnetby et W. Stanlowe. xvli vjd

SUMMA TOTALIS RECEPTE CCCCXXXIJli VIJs XJd

De quibus

[1] *Sic.*

Allocaciones superplusagii compoti precedentis (Marg.)

Idem computat in superplusagio ultimi compoti sui finiente xv^mo^ die Februarii anno Regis nunc xij^mo^ prout patet in pede ibidem. xj^li^ xij^s^ iiij^d^ ob

Summa xj^li^ vij^s^ iiij^d^ obolus

Custus edificii castri de Tateshale (Marg.)

Empcio petrarum (Marg.)

(Idem)^c^ ^i^ Et computat in diversis misis custibus et expensis factis ac impositis super operibus castri predicti per tempus compoti prout per particulas in quodam quaterno papiri inde confecto super compotum ostenso et examinato (evidenter apparet)^c^ ac inter huiusmodi compoti memoranda remanente evidenter apparet vicelicet in D^ma^ lx petris liberis ^lxxiiijs iiijd^ emptis in querrura de ^ccc petris^ Willesford, ^clx^ Hesilbargh et ^c^ma^^ Skowpe precio singule centene xiij^s^ iiij^d^. Centena ^xiijs iiijd^ petris emptis (de) in querrura de Asshby ix ^vs vd^ petris vocatis perpontasshelers (emptis cont')^c^ continentibus xxxvj pedes precio singuli pedis ij^d^ ob. ^ijs viijd^ iiijor petris vocatis formepeces continentibus viij pedes precio singuli pedis iiij^d^ emptis in dicta querrura de Hesilbargh ^iiijs^ cariagio earundarum petrarum vocatarum perpontasshelers et formepeces a dicta querrura (usque)^i^ Waynegate. ^vs xd^ xiij petris vocatis odgyfes continentibus xlvij pedes precio singuli pedis j d. ob. emptis in dicta querrura de Skowpe et denariis solutis ballivo domini de Kyme pro ^ijs iijd^ passagio habendo ad cariandum dictorum ccccix asshelers proveniencium a querruriis de Willesford et Hesilbargh (videlicet singula centena ad vj^d^)^i^ omnibus simul computatis. cvi^s^ x^d^

Cariagium petrarum (Marg.)

Et in custu apposito super cariagio earundem petrarum usque castrum predictum prout in dicto quaterno plenius apparet una cum xiij^s^ j^d^ solutis pro cariagio cx^ma^ petrarum liberarum vocatorum sandston' emptarum de Johanne Kighley apud querruram de Salmondby etc.[1] viijli xiijs ixd

Stipendia cementariorum (Marg.)

Et in feodis et vadiis (diversorum)[1] cementariorum operancium super operibus predictis per tempus compoti videlicet Petri Mason [xijs viijd] Johannis [lxxs] Mason Roberti [vijli ixs xid] Mason Johannis [xiijs] Boteler et ij serviencium [xxs ijd] suorum. Johannis [iiijs viijd] Mason de Waynflet Roberti Mason [vs vjd] de comitatu Ebor' et Thome Gemme [vs vjd] prout in dicto quaterno apercius annotatur. xiiijli xvijd

Empcio et factura tegularum vocatarum Waltile (Marg.)

Et in custu apposito super factura (et) combustura et cariagio DLml tegularum vocatarum waltile hoc anno factarum apud torale tegulinum domini super Edlyngton More una cum xjli solutis in plenam solucionem facture DCma huiusmodi tegularum anno precedente factarum ut in eodem quaterno particulariter patet. cxvli xiijs vjd

Et in huiusmodi custu apposito super empcione et cariagio tegularum vocatarum waltile proveniencium de exitu consimilis toralis tegulini domini apud Boston ut in eodem quaterno plenius apparet. cxvs iiijd

Stipendia cementariorum vocatorum Brekemasons (Marg.)

Et in mercede (diversorum)[1] cementariorum vocatorum Brekemasons et eorum serviencium operancium super operibus diversis modis ibidem per tempus compoti sicut in dicto quaterno evidencius continetur. lli xiijs xd ob.

Stipendia cementariorum vocatorum Rughmasons (Marg.)

Et in mercede Johannis Ramsey sociorum et serviencium eius vocatorum Rughmasons operancium in diversis operibus ibidem per

[1] *Sic.*

tempus predictum ut in eodem quaterno particulariter intitulatur. xv^{li} xv^{s} iij^{d}

Custus calcee vive (Marg.)

Et in custo apposito super combustione x toralium (cl)^{c} calsis vive per tempus predictum una cum petris et focali emptis ad idem opus prout lucidius in dicto quaterno liquet. xix^{li} $xviij^{s}$ vij^{d}

Emptio et cariagium maeremii (Marg.)

Et in custu apposito super empcione et cariagio maeremii bosci empti per tempus predictum (tam)^{c} super dictis operibus tam (apud)^{c} in bosco Abbatis de Bardney (xviij*li* xiij*s* vij*d*) quam in bosco de Thornton (iiij*li* xviij*s* x*d*) et alibi prout in eodem quaterno apparet. $xxiij^{li}$ $xiij^{s}$ v^{d}

Custus unius fumarii aule (Marg.)

Et in custu apposito super nova fabricione unius fumarii hoc anno facti ex maeremii (domini) proveniencis de bosco domini apud Elinton per tempus compoti. Ut pro aula castri predicti sicut in dicto quaterno evidenter continetur. cj^{s} ij^{d}

Stipendia carpentariorum (Marg.)

Et in mercede et stipendiis diversorum carpentariorum operancium super operibus carpentrie ibidem per tempus (compoti)^{c} predictum sicut in dicto quaterno de singulorum nominibus plene liquet. $xiiij^{li}$ xviii^{s} $iiij^{d}$

Stipendia junctorum (Marg.)

Et in huiusmodi mercede Roberti Kerver et socii eius operancium (ibidem)^{c}. Ut in syling parlure et alibi ibidem per idem tempus sicut (in)[1] dicto quaterno plenius specificatur. $liiij^{s}$ iij^{d}

Carracio tabularum (Marg.)

Et in custu apposito super carracione tabularum per tempus predictum ut in mercede Johannis Fyssher et aliorum (oper)^{c} sociorum(p)^{c} eius prout in eodem quaterno particulariter intitulatur. xix^{s} xi^{d}

Custus palicii fossati castri (Marg.)

Et in denariis solutis super carriagio et factura palicii situati desuper ripam exterioris fossati ex parte occidentali castri hoc anno prout in eodem quaterno liquet. xl^{s} vj^{d}

Empcio et caragium tabularum (Marg.)

Et in cc^{ma} $^{\text{vij}\,li}$ tabularum vocatorum waynscott' proveniencium de providencia domini apud Hull precio singule vij^{d} $^{\text{x}s\ \text{v}d}$ cariagium earundem usque le Newdike et xij $^{\text{xxiiij}s\ \text{vj}d}$ tabulis vocatis plaunchers emptis apud Newerk cum cariagio ut in eodem quaterno patet. viij^{li} xiiij^{s} xi^{d}

Empcio ferri non operati (Marg.)

Et in xviij gaddis j garba de Osmondez et v pecibus de foldynyryn et ij paribus ligaturarum ferri vocatis wyndowlandez emptis ad idem opus per tempus compoti ad diversa precia sicut in eodem (libro)[c] quaterno plenius monstratur. lxxvij^{s} ix^{d}

Empcio ferri operati (Marg.)

Et in ceruris ligaturis hamis et huiusmodi minutis necessariis ferri emptis de Johanne Loksmyth de Conyngesby ad opus predictum per idem tempus prout in dicto quaterno particulariter apparet. xviij^{s}

Fabricacio ferramenti (Marg.)

Et in denariis solutis dicto Johanni Smyth de Conyngesby, Radulpho Smith, Willelmo Smyth et Johanni Smyth de Tateshale pro fabricacione diversorum ferramentorum ad idem opus per tempus compoti sicut in eodem quaterno plenius liquet. iiij^{li} vi^{d}

Empcio clavorum (Marg.)

Et in M^{l}D $^{\text{viij}s\ \text{vj}d}$ clavis vocatis grete spikengs M^{l}cccc $^{\text{iiij}s\ \text{viij}d}$ clavis vocatis midilspikengs M^{l}M^{l}M^{l}M^{l}D $^{\text{ix}s\ \text{iiij}d}$ clavis vocatis staknayle xiiij M^{l} $^{\text{xvij}s\ \text{vj}d}$ latnayle, et M^{l}M^{l}M^{l} $^{\text{ij}s\ \text{vj}d}$ latisnayle emptis ad opus predictum per idem tempus prout in dicto quaterno apparet. xli^{s} vj^{d}

Custus operis plumbi (Marg.)

xxvj*s* viij*d*
Et in regardo dato Johanni Plommer et
xviij*d*
servientibus suis Waltero Plummer (et)[c]
operantibus et reficientibus diversa opera
x*s* iij*d*
plumbi ibidem una cum xlj libris sawder ad
ix*s*
idem opus et stipendium cuiusdam hominis
mundantis cineres plumbi etc.[1] ut in eodem
quaterno patet. xlvij^{s} v^{d}

Empcio vitri operati (Marg.)

m iiij*li* iv*s* xx*s*
Et in c xij pedibus vitri ad ix^{d} et xv scutis
vitri ad xvj^{d} emptis de Thoma Sturdwike de
Boston pro fenestris parlure camere desuper
et ex parte occidentali aule prout evidencius
in eodem quaterno apparet. ciiij^{s}

Empcio et cariagium plastri (Marg.)

xxxvj*s*
Et in xxxvj doliis plastri Parisiensis emptis
xxj*dol* xv
apud Gaynesburgh et Granby ad opus pre-
iiij*li* vj*s* vij*d*
dictum precio singulorum xij^{d} cariagio et
iiij*li* iiij*d*
operacione huiusmodi plastri ut in eodem
quaterno particulariter demonstratur. x^{li} ij^{s} xj^{d}

Cariagium tegularum, zabuli, petrarum et huiusmodi (Marg.)

Et in mercede diversorum cariancium (cum
carecta sua)[1] petras tegulas zabulum et huius-
modi ad idem opus per tempus predictum
vij*li* x*s* iiij*d* ma xx
videlicet Johannis Bonour per c iiij dies
xxxij*s* viiij*d*
dimidium ad ix^{d} Thome Childe per xlix dies
xj*s* iiij*d*
Ricardi Baker per xvij dies ad viij^{d} et
xij*s* viij*d*
Ricardi Ermyt per xxxviij dies ad iiij^{d} ut in
(eodem (libro)[c] quaterno patet)[1]. x^{li} vij^{s}

Stipendia laborariorum (Marg.)

xxxvij*s* vj*d* xxxvij*s*
Et in stipendiis Ricardi Sawer, Roberti
vj*d*
Tiler laborariorum conductorum per annum
utroque ad xxx^{s} ut pro v terminis infra

[1] *Sic.*

tempus compotum accidentibus (et)[c] ac Roberti Wilkynson (xxviijs iijd) et aliorum laborariorum operancium in diversis operibus ibidem ut in dicto quaterno annotatur. ciij[s] iij[d]

Escuracio et evacuacio fossati castri (Marg.)

Et in mercede Mathei Dyker et sociorum eius operancium super escuracione et aque evacuacione fossatorum in circuitu castri predicti (per inter xxv)[c] quasi pro stipendio unius hominis per c[m] lxiij dies incipientes xxviij[o] die Marcii anno xiij[mo] et continuandos usque primum diem in clauso compoti capientes per diem v[d] ad tascam prout particulariter et diatim in quodam quaterno penes (ipsum computantem)[1] remanente (evidenter)[c] liquet. lxxvj[s] iij[d]

Empcio batellarum cum stipendiis famularium ad easdem (Marg.)

Et in duabus (viijli xiijs iiijd) batellis per dominum emptis mense Decembris infra tempus compoti pro suo cariagio ad opus predictum faciendo una cum mercede Johannis (xxxixs iiijd) Drawall et aliorum conductorum ad cariandum petras tegulas et (necessaria)[c] alia necessaria ad opus predictum cum eisdem batellis (ac aliis (xijs ixd) minutis emptis pro eisdem batellis indigentibus)[1] sicut in dicto quaterno inter memoranda huius compoti remanente plenius (apparet)[c] continetur. xj[li] v[s] v[d]

Custus deposicionis domorum in abbatia de Revesby (Marg.)

Et in custu apposito super deposicione domorum per dominum emptorum in abbatia de Revesby per tempus compoti ut in expensis (vjs (viijd)[c]) carpentariorum et aliorum laborariorum expensis (xxjd) solutis super cariagio xiij carectatarum maeremii de prece et expensis (ijs vijd) tam serviencium domini quam aliorum superveniencium de prece cariancium xj[ml] ccc[ma]lx tegulas vj ostia et x fenestras provenientes de eisdem domibus sicut in eodem quaterno apparet. x[s] iiij[d]

Expense necessarie (Marg.)

Et in denariis solutis super variis solucionibus misis et expensis necessariis tangentibus (opus tocius)^{c} diversis operibus infra castrum et ad usum eiusdem per tempus compoti perpetratis prout per ij titulos (infra)^{c} in eodem quaterno annotatos particulariter apparet quorum, primus continet xxiiij^{s} iiij^{d} et secundus lxxj^{s} iij^{d} etc.[1] iiij^{li} xv^{s} vij^{d}

Allocaciones mense operariorum (Marg.)

Et in allocacione facta eidem computanti pro mensa diversorum operariorum operancium super operibus predictis in hospicio domini existencium (vide)^{c} inter xv^{m} diem Februarii in principio compoti et crastinum sancti Michaelis archangeli extunc proximum sequentem prout in compoto Johannis Crakehall clerici extunc temporis eiusdem hospicii custodis (plenius apparet)^{c} finiente eodem crastino sancti Michaelis plene liquet et ut habeat allocacionem tot denariorum superius oneratorum pro huiusmodi mensa etc.[1] xviij^{li} iij^{s} viij^{d}

ccclxxvj^{li} xv^{s} vij^{d} ob.

SUMMA CCCLXXVJ^{li} XV^{s} VII^{d} OB.

Custus fossacionis et escuracionis fossati (Marg.)

Et in denariis solutis Matheo Diker conducto ad faciendum de novo xxxvj rodas fossati incipientis a cursu aque de Bayne et linialiter discendentis[1] quasi per medium mercati de Tateshale usque quandam portam caducam vocatam le Baryate capienti pro singula roda ex certa convencione secum facta per Robertum Gowshill, rectorem de Cromwell xx^{d}. lx^{s}

Et in denariis solutis eidem Matheo Diker in partem solucionis xli^{li} xiij^{s} iiij^{d} sibi per dominum concessis ut pro (nova)^{c} fossacione cc^{ma} x rodarum cuiusdam fossati de novo facti incipiencis a dicta porta vocata Baryate et sic descendentis usque ad finem orientem alterius fossati vocati le Newdike capienti pro singula

[1] *Sic.*

roda (continent' in latitudine et profunditate)^c. iij^s iiij^d xx^{li} xiij^s iiij^d

Et solutum eidem Matheo (conducto)^c pro fossacione ccc^{ma} xl rodarum novi fossati vocati le Wardike ex parte occidentali (eiusdem)^c dictarum cc^{ma} x rodarum (pro)^c ex ordinacione domini capienti pro singula roda vd. viij^{li} vj^s viij^d

Et in custu apposito super cariagio (subbosci, boscalis ad haias inde faciendas)^c (et factura haiarum desuper)[1] dicto fossato vocato le Wardyke videlicet in mercede Willelmi$^{xs\ vjd}$ Chapman et socii eius cariancium xlij carectarum salicum a diversis locis infra dominium (de Tateshale)[1] prostratarum capientium pro singula carectata iij^d, mercede Simonis Lang$^{vijs\ vid}$ (cariantis)^c et socii eius cariancium xviij carectas spinarum extra parcum chacee domini qualibet carecta ad vd, mercede, eiusdem Simonis et socii eius cariancium DLX$^{ixs\ ijd}$ faggotorum vocatorum hegyngkiddes a bosco domini vocato Kirkbywode capientium pro singula centena xxd, et in stipendio Willelmi Peccham$^{xxxiijs\ ivd}$ et socii eius de novo facientium ccc^{ma} xl rodas haiarum desuper positarum dicto fossato vocato le Wardike qualibet roda ad jd omnibus simul computatis ut patet in predicto quaterno remanente etc.[1] lx^s vj^d

Et in denariis solutis dicto Matheo Diker pro elargacione et escuracione c^{ma} lv rodarum fossati (d)^c incipiencis a quadam porta vocata le Neweyate ex parte occidentali clausi domini vocati Mikilhardclos usque seweram aque de Wythom capienti pro singula roda viij^d ex certa convencione secum facta per Johannem Fulnetby una cum iij^s iiij^d sibi concessis per dominum de regardo vi^{li}

Et solutis Johanni Pranke pro factura xxx rodarum haie nuncupate fotehegge facte in diversis locis desuper ripam eiusdem fossati locis magis indigentibus propter aque effluxum etc.[1] qualibet roda ad j^d. ij^s viij^d

SUMMA XLI^{li} IIJ^s IJ^d

[1] *Sic.*

Allocationes forinsece (Marg.)

Respondit anno futuro de precis istorum fagottorum (Marg.)

Et in allocacione facta eidem computanti in precio M^{l}c^{ma}lx faggottorum de parte xv^{ml}c^{ma}xxiiij fagottorum proveniencium de bosco et subbosco (succisis)[1] in bosco domini vocato Stikeswoldsouthwode per tempus compoti superius (alloc)^{c} non allocatorum eo quod nondum exponuntur (die)^{c} super combustione tegularum (set remanent super ripam aque de Witham)[1] precio singule centene ij^{s} iiij^{d} (una secundum)^{c} prout superius oneratur una cum vij^{s} viij^{d} solutis pro (cariagio)^{c} factura eorundem fagottorum videlicet pro singula centena viij^{d}. xxxiiij^{s} vj^{d}

Et in factura M^{l}dc iiij^{xx}vj fagottorum accidencium Priorisse de Stikeswold ut pro decima xvj^{ml}dccc^{ma} fagottorum factorum in bosco predicto precio facture singule centene viij^{d}. xi^{s} ij^{d}

Et in mercede Willelmi Rokeray et socii eius cariancium dictos M^{l}c^{ma}lx fagottos a dicto bosco usque predictam ripam aque de Wythom capientium pro singula centena iiij^{d} maius in toto pro regardo ijd ex certa convencione facta per Johannem Tailboys etc.[1] iiij^{s}

xviij*s* viij*d*

Et in denariis solutis Johanni Warner et

xii*s*

Willelmo Peper carpentariis in partem solucionis veteris debiti eius per dominum debiti de tempore quo Robertus Gowshill (clericus)^{c} extitit (clericus)^{c} supervisor operum castri predicti ex mandato domini prout super compotum satis attestatum est. xxx^{s} viij^{d}

(Summa xlix^{s} viij^{d})^{c}

xlix^{s} viij^{d} (*Marg.*)

Summa iiij^{li} iiij^{d}

Expense necessarie (Marg.)

Et in pergameno empto apud Lincoln per Robertum Broun pro compoto ipsius computantis finienti xv^{mo} die Februarii anno xij^{mo} desuper scribendo. xvj^{d}

[1] *Sic.*

Et in v quaternis papiri emptis tam per parcellas ipsius computantis quam compoto isto desuper scribendo precio singuli, iiij^{d} xx^{d}

ii*s* v*s*

Et in expensis una carectata feni et iij quarteriarum avenarum emptarum super sustentacione equi ipsius computantis per

xij*d*

tempus compoti una cum ferrura eiusdem equi simul computata. viij^{s}

Et in expensis ipsius computantis per quatuor vices infra tempus compoti equitantis

xvj*d*

usque Cromwell pro pecuniis de rectore ibidem recipiendis, alia vice mense Augusti equitantis

v*d*

usque Boston ad providendum (se)^{c} et emendum ferrum Ispannie et vj chalderas carbon-

ix*d*

um (hui)^{c} alia vice mense Decembris anno xiijo itinerantis a Tateshale usque Lincoln ad deferendam literam domini directam domino Willelmo Derby canonico ecclesie Cathedralis

viij*d*

ibidem et expensis ipsius et Johannis Warner mense Octobris eodem anno xiij^{mo} itinerancium usque Kyme ad eligendum et providendum de xx arboribus quercubus ibidem per dominum emptis pro focali suo habendis, omnibus simul computatis. iij^{s} ij^{d}

(xiij^{s} ij^{d})^{c} (Marg.)

Summa xiiij^{s} ij^{d}

Stipendium computantis (Marg.)

Et in feodo ipsius computantis cause officii sui ad liij^{s} iiij^{d} per annum solvendo terminis Pasche sanctorum Botulphi, Michaelis et Nativitatis domini prout allocatum est in compoto precedente videlicet pro huiusmodi v terminis infra tempus compoti accidentibus. lxvj^{s} viij^{d}

(lxviij^{s} viij^{d})

Summa lxvj^{s} viij^{d}

Liberaciones denariorum (Marg.)
Respondet ballivus de Tateshale (Marg.)

Et in denariis liberatis Thome Cowper ballivo domini de Tateshale ut in tot denariis solutis pro diversis operibus tangentibus officium dicti ballivi ultra xix^{li} vj^{s} ij^{d} obstupatos pro pecuniis receptis de exitu officii eiusdem ballivi (videlicet)[c] prout in compoto suo finiente in festo sancti Michaelis anno xiij^{o} evidenter apparet. vi^{li} v^{s} viij^{d}

Respondet firmarius de Snawdon (Marg.)

Et in huiusmodi denariis libertatis firmario terre dominicalis de Snawdon ut in custu
iiij*li* xl*s*
fossati per manus Mathei Diker et Baldewini
xvj*d*
Brekeman cum adquisitione vininum ad idem opus ut in compoto ibidem finiente in dicto festo Michaelis patet. vi^{li} xvj^{d}

Respondet R. Leper (Marg.)

Et liberavit Roberto Leper venditori bosci
xiij*s* iiij*d*
domini apud Tumby tam super factura
xx*s*
fagottorum ibidem quam per manus Johannis Kighley ut in denariis per ipsum (Johannem)[1] receptis de Willelmo Stanlowe mense Januarii anno xiij^{o}. xxxiij^{s} iv^{d}

Respondet J. Crakehall (Marg.)

Et liberavit Johanni Crakehall clerico nuper custodi (hospicii)[1] domini denarios recipienti (ut)[c] in precio diversorum victualium et aliarum solucionum pro eodem hospicio per ipsum computantem factarum prout tam per particulas in dicto quaterno papiri annotatas quam in compoto ipsius Johannis finiente in crastino sancti Michaelis apparet. xix^{s} ix^{d}

(xv^{li} i d)[c] (Marg.)

Summa xv^{li} j^{d}

Dorse : m.4 beginning at the lower edge.
(Mise cccl^{li} xvj^{s} ix^{d} excedit xvij^{li} viij^{s} x^{d})[c] (Marg.)

SUMMA OMNIUM SOLUCIONUM EXPENSARUM ALLOCACIONUM ET LIBERACIONUM PREDICTARUM—CCCCLII^{li} VIJ^{s} V^{d} (xvj^{s} ix^{d})[c] (*Marg.*)

Et sic reprise excedunt recepta superius onerata per xix^{li} xix^{s} vi^{d} (xviij^{li} viij^{s} x^{d})[c]
Qui allocantur in compoto anni subsequentis.

Respectur' (Marg. with bracket to include all entries to p. 17, line 2).

Ei–lx^{s} pro tot denariis liberatis Baldewino Brekeman de prefato super factura cccc^{ml} tegularum (nondum combustarum)[1] per talliam super compotum ostensurum usque proximum compotum.

Eidem—xiij^{s} iiij^{d} pro tot denariis solutis tam
xs
Johanni Swayne pro M^{l} garbarum cooperi-
iiis iiijd
menti quam Willelmo Forster de parte viij^{s}
iiij^{d} sibi debitorum pro cariagio zabuli super factura dictarum cccc^{ma} tegularum etc.[1] usque proximum compotum.

Eidem—xxvij^{s} iiij^{d} pro tot denariis solutis
xiijs iiijd
tam super factura fagottorum proveniencium de ij acris dimidia bosce emptis de Johanne Hert in bosco de Bardney quam in denariis
xs (xiiiis)[c]
solutis Thome Lang de Conyngesby et fratri
iiijs
suo ac Willelmo Borell pro cariagio maeremii provenientis de eisdem ij acris dimidia bosce ac sic in respectu posito usque proximum compotum.

(Cancellatum quia allocatum est superius)[1]

xviiis viiid
(Eidem—xxx^{s} viij^{d} pro tot denariis solutis Johanni Warner et
xiis
Willelmo Peper in parte carpentar' in partem solucionis veteris debiti sibi debiti de tempore quo Robertus Gowshill nuper ibidem extitit clericus operum castri predicti quousque habeatur warrantum etc.)[c]

Eidem—iij^{s} iij^{d} (solutis Johanni)[c] soluendis Johanni Betson pro cariagio xxviii (pl)[c] tabularum vocatarum plaunchers proveniencium de bosco domini apud Elinton videlicet pro huiusmodi cariagio earundem a Lincoln usque fossatum iuxta Tateshale vocatum le Mersshedike usque proximum compotum.

Eidem—xlv^{s} pro tot denariis currendis in onere Ricardi Frith (immediate)[c] custodis hospicii domini ut in pacacione facta (tam)[1] Johanni Grene et socio suo in plenam solucionem lx^{s} convencionis sue pro prostracione et fissura xx veterum quercorum emptorum per dominum in bosco de Kyme pro focali (habendo)[c] habendo ad usum dicti hospicii ultra xx^{s} pre manibus solutos eidem Johanni ut de exitu recepte dicti Ricardi extra coffrum domini, quam in
vs
huiusmodi solucione facta Ricardo Hieghege et Thome socio suo mense Decembris anno xiij^{mo} continuanda per (xvj)[c] xv dies super combustione carbonum boscalium in bosco domini vocato

[1] *Sic.*

Kirkbywode capientibus per diem ad mensam domini iiij^{d} sic hic in respectu positum usque dictum proximum compotum etc.

Respect' viij^{li} xix^{s} viij^{d}

Habet superplusagium clarum cum respectis xxvij^{li} viij^{s} vj^{d} (Marg.)

In manibus computantis xlvij^{s} viij^{d} (Marg.)

Unde ostenduntur nomina creditorum per billam continentem xxix^{li} xvj^{s} ij^{d} et hiis itaque oneratis quasi recepta et soluta per coffrum domini restant.

[membrane 3]

Nomina creditorum operum.

Debentur (Marg.) in centre of bracket.

Thome Perch' de Conyngesby xxvj*s* v*s* viij*d* pro maeremio et clavis ab eo emptis ad usum operum predictorum per tempus compoti.	xxxi^{s} viij^{d}	
Johanni Lowys de Boston pro xj gaddez ferri Ispannie et v peciis ferri vocatis faldynyron ab eo emptis ad opera predicta per iij vices.	xlvij^{s} ij^{d}	
Rogero Barker de Boston pro iij xj*s* iiij*d* xxliij*s* gaddez ferri Ispannie, vj chalderis carbonum maritimorum. Cariagio xliij*s* cum portagio xij chalderum huius- ij*s* iij*d* modi carbonum ac portagio v^{ml} tegularum simul computatis.	lxxix^{s} vij^{d}	Assignatur
Thome Tilehouse pro cariagio x millenarum tegularum de Boston usque Tateshale mensibus Decembris et Aprilis anno xiij^{o} millena ad xvj^{d}.	xiij^{s} iv^{d}	
Thome Stoyle pro cariagio petrarum ultra xx^{s} sibi solutos per ballivum de Welby, etc.[1]	vi^{li} xx^{d}	
Johanni Betson de Lincoln pro diversis cariagiis usque Tateshale, etc.[1]	xi^{li} ix^{s} ix^{d}	
Willelmo Forster de Stikeswold pro cariagio fagottorum ad torale domini tegulinum, etc.[1]	xxij^{s} ij^{d}	

[1] *Sic.*

Johanni Warner carpentario pro vadiis suis aretro	xxxvij^{s} x^{d}	Assignatur
Thome Toly carpentario de parte feodi sui	ij^{s}	
Ricardo othe Hill carpentario de parte feodi sui.	ij^{s}	
Johanni Moller de parte vadiorum suorum	ij^{s}	
Johanni Thomson de Tumby pro cariagio unius carecte spinarum.	x^{d}	
Johanni Donour pro cariagio usque castrum, etc.[1]	vj^{s} ij^{d}	

Summa creditorum xxix^{li} xvj^{s} ij^{d}

[Membrane 2^{d} is blank.]

[Membrane 1^{d} beginning at the other end.]

Compotus Thome Croxby operum Radulphi Domini Cromwell castri sui de Tateshal supervisoris finiens secundo die Maii anno H. sexti xiij^{mo}....xiij^{mo}....xiij^{mo}.... ....Croxby.........castri de Tateshale finient' secundo die maii anno H. sexti xiij^{o}

Tegule minoris forme facte anno x^{mo} (Marg. with bracket covering two entries).

Infrascriptus computans respondet de c^{ml}D tegulis (minoris forme)[1] vocatis waltile factis apud torale domini tegulinum super Edlyngton More anno Regis nunc x^{mo} de remanentia (ut)^{c} quarum quelibet formatur in longitudine ix pollicum latitudine iiij pollicum dimidii et in spissitudine ij pollicum et iiij partium pollicis ut in (proximo)[1] compoto precedente plenius annotatur. De huiusmodi tegulis per tempus compoti non respondet quia nulle de consimili forma set de maiori facta fuerunt ut in[fra]

Summa c^{ml}d De quibus

..*Abbas de Kirkstede* (Marg.)

Idem computat fore (dat')^{c} (liberatum)[1] Abbati de Kirkestede de parte maioris numeri sibi per dominum (dat')^{c} (assignati)[1] ut asseritur per eundem computantem sine warranto, xxxv ^{ml}cccc.

Abbas de Bardney (Marg.)

Et liberatum Abbati de Bardney ex huiusmodi (dono)^{c} (assignatione)[1] domini in partem (maioris numeri vii^{ml})^{c} xx^{ml} per litteram de warranto viij^{ml}.

[1] *Sic.*

Et exponuntur super (diversis)[1] operibus Castri de Tateshale per scrutinium quaterni ipsius computantis liij^{ml}.

Summa misa $\overset{xx}{\text{iiij}}$ xvj^{ml} cccc centene. Et remanent M^{l}M^{l}M^{l}M^{l}c, unde apud

{ Tilehous M^{l}M^{l}ccc
{ Mersshdike M^{l}Dccc

Tegule maioris forme facte annis xjmo et xijmo. Respondet dictus Abbas de Bardney. (Marg. with bracket covering two entries.)

Et respondit de D^{m}iiij^{xx}vij^{ml} (huiusmodi)[c] tegulis vocatis waltile maioris forme factis anno xjmo (ut)[c] de remanentia quarum qualibet formatur in long[itudine] x pollicum latitudine v pollicum et spissitudine ij pollicum dimidii ut in (dicto)[1] compoto precedente evidenter apparet. Et de D^{ml}l^{ml} (huius modi)[c] tegulis huiusmodi forme factis per tempus compoti ut patet infra.

Summa xjc^{m} xxxvij^{ml} De quibus

Idem computans fore liberatum predicto Abbati de Bardney de prestito ex mandato domini ut asseritur per Baldewinum Brekeman sine warranto xii^{ml}.

Et exponuntur super operibus castri predicti per tempus compoti ut liquet per examinacionem super compotum—ccc^{ml} xliij^{ml} Dc^{ml}

Summa misa ccc^{ml} lvij^{m} Dc^{m}

Et remanent Dcc^{ml} lxxix^{m} cccc^{m}, unde apud

{ (unde apud)[c]
{ Torale tegulinum D^{m}xxix^{ml} cccc^{m}
{ Mersshdike cc^{ml}l^{ml}

II

13th April, 1438—31st May, 1439

Officium Clerici operum Castri de Tateshale (Marg.)

COMPOTUS THOME CROXBY SUPERVISORIS OPERUM RADULPHI DOMINI CROMWELL CASTRI SUI DE TATESHALE A FESTO PASCHE ACCIDENTE XIIJ^{MO} DIE APRILIS ANNO REGNI REGIS HENRICI SEXTI XVJ^{MO} USQUE ULTIMUM DIEM MAII ANNO EIUSDEM REGIS XVIJ^{MO} PER UNUM ANNUM INTEGRUM ET XLVIIJ DIES.

Arreragia (Marg.)

Idem respondet de—xvij^{li} xiiij^{s} x^{d} ob. de arreragiis ultimi compoti anni proxime precedentis prout patet in pede ibidem.

Summa—xvij^{li} xiiij^{s} x^{d} ob.

Recepta denariorum de generali receptore domini (Marg.)

Et de cclj^{li} iij^{d} ob. receptis de Willelmo Stanlowe Receptore domini generali per manus diversorum ministrorum domini in comitatu Lincoln...alibi super operibus castri predicti per tempus compoti prout tam in compoto ipsius generalis Receptoris quam in compotis eorumdem ministrorum....ad festum sancti Michaelis anno Regis nunc xvij^{mo} particulariter continetur. Simul cum xx^{li} receptis de Henrico Coote de denariis . . . bosci et subbosci in Tumby hoc anno.

examinatur Summa cclj^{li} iij^{d} ob.

Vendicio tegularum et fagottorum (Marg.)

Et de viij^{s} vj^{d} de precio M^{l}dcc tegularum maioris forme vocatarum waltyle venditarum Rogero Prestes hoc anno ut d . . . Ml v^{s}. Et de xj^{li} viij^{s} ix^{d} de precio xiij^{ml} vij xxx^{cma} fagottorum hoc anno succisorum in bosco domini vocato Stikswod S . . . . pro expensis thoralis domini apud Edlyngton ut extra precium centene xx^{d}

examinatur Summa xi^{li} xvij^{s} iij^{d}.

Recepta denariorum de cofris domini (Marg.)

Et de xlvij^{li}, receptis de cofris domini per manus diversorum videlicet Johannis [vi^{li} xiij^{s} iiij^{d}] Croke xiij^{mo} die Junii anno xvj^{mo} Ricardi W [xvj^{li} xiij^{s}] . . . . ad duas vices unde prima vice in vigilia Pentecostes anno xvj^{mo} x^{li} et secunda vice xxix^{mo} die Augusti eodem anno vj^{li} xiij^{s} iiij^{d} Johannis Tamworth [xx^{li} vj^{s} viij^{d}] ad duas vices prima vice in vigilia Pentecostes eodem anno vij^{li} et secunda vice in vigilia Pasche anno xvij^{mo} xiij^{li} vj^{s} viij^{d} et Willelmi Stanlowe [lxvj^{s} viij^{d}] in festo Pasche anno xvij^{mo} predicto per parcellas prefato modo testatas. Et de x^{li} xiij^{s} iiij^{d} receptis de eisdem cofris domini ad manus Baldewyni Brekman ad iij vices unde prima

cs xxs
vice per manus Willelmi Stanlowe apud London et Tateshale vj^{li} : secunda vice per manus Ricardi Westby apud Cheswyke xxvj^{s} viij^{d} et tercia vice per manus Petri Idle lxvj^{s} viij^{d} Et de xls receptis de eisdem cofris domini ad manus Godfridi Brekman apud London in principio convencionis et retencionis sue cum domino in parte solucionis iiij^{li} de huiusmodi integra convencione sua per indenturam suam etc.[1]

examinatur Summa lix^{li} xiij^{s} iiij^{d}.

Relaxacio denariorum per creditores (Marg.)

Et de lv^{s} de denariis per Johannem Betson unum creditorem istius officij tam anni precedentis quam huius anni relaxatis pro cer . . . . solucione habenda de denariis sibi per dominum debitis ex mera et propria recognitione computantis super hunc compotum.

examinatur Summa lv^{s}.

SUMMA TOTALIS RECEPTE CUM ARRERAGIIS CCCXLIII^{li} IX^{d}.

Superplusagium (Marg.)

De quibus computat in superplusagio istius computantis ultimi compoti sui anni proxime precedentis prout patet in pede ibidem xj^{li} xij^{s} iiij^{d} Summa xj^{li} xij^{s} iiij^{d}.

Custus edificii domorum et aliarum infra castrum predictum (Marg.)

Et in diversis custibus misis et expensis factis ac appositis super operibus Castri de Tateshale per totum tempus huius compoti sicut per parcellas in quodam quaterno papiri confecto super compotum ostensas et particulariter examinatas ac inter memoranda eiusdem remanente evidenter et particulariter continetur videlicet
viij*li* ix*s* vij*d* viij*li* xix*s* iiij*d*
in petris liberis emptis . cariagio earundem petrarum . stipendiis
xxij*li* vij*s* ij*d* lxix*li* v*s* j*d* ob. c
lathomorum, custus facture cccc^{ml} iiij^{xx} x^{ml} vij t . . . vocatarum
xvij*li* xvj*s* iiij*d*
waltile factarum per Foys Brekmaker . denariis persolutis Baldewyno Brekmaker super custu facture viij^{ml} huiusmodi tegularum, cariagio
xxi*li* x*s* ij*d*
dictarum tegularum factarum per Foys Brekmaker empcione
iiij*li* x*d* ob.
huiusmodi tegularum ad thorale domini apud Boston cum cariagio
xlvij*li* xiiij*d*
earundem . stipendiis cementariorum vocatorum Brekmasons,
xviiij*li* xiij*s* x*d*
stipendio Johannis Ramsey et sociorum suorum vocatorum Rough-
xxix*li* xj*s* vj*d*
brekmasons. stipendio Mathei Dyker et sociorum suorum evacuantium fundamentum de le Countremure, magni stabuli et aliarum
xlij*li* xvj*s* v*d*
domorum ibidem . custu facture calcis vive cum empcione petrarum

[1] *Sic.*

xxijli vs viijd
et carbonum pro eadem cum cariagio, empcione maeremij in bosco
Abbatis de Bardney cum cariagio . ac cariagio huiusmodi maeremij
xxxvli iiijs vjd
de bosco de Braunceton . stipendio carpentariorum stipendio
xlvjs iiijd iiijli xixs ixd iiijli xijs vijd
sarratorum . empcione ferii Ispanie . fabricacione ferramentorum
lxxijs ijd ixs xli iijd
de eodem . empcione clavorum . empcione vitri . empcione plastri
ciiijs viijd
Parisiensis cum cariagio . stipendio laborariorum cum mensa servien-
xli xxd
cium . cariagio tegularum calcis zabuli et huiusmodi de aqua in
lijs viiid
Castrum et extra Castrum . custibus batellarum domini cum stipen-
dio laborariorum cariancium cum eisdem batellis . empcione neces-
lijs iiijd vijli iijs vd ob.
sariorum pro operibus infra castrum, custibus appositis super
paccacione tocius lane domini infra idem castrum ultra xxxv^s
xvjli ixs ijd
solutis per Eliam Warde . factura et mundacione fossatorum diversis
cjs vid xs ijd
locis . factura haiarum et sepum in pluribus locis. Custibus factis
iiijli xs iiijd
infra manerium de Whitehall. Solucionibus et minutis expensis
cxiijs viijd
neccessariis . custibus plumbi cum operacione eiusdem . in toto
per parcellas prefato modo testatas, etc.[1]

Examinatur Summa cccc xxxiiij^li xvi^d ob.

Feoda et vadia (Marg.)

Et in feodo ipsius computantis causa officii sui per annum prout allocatum est in compoto precedente liij^s iiij^d. Et in vadiis eiusdem computantis per xxj septimanas inter xxvij^mum diem Junii et xij diem Decembris ambo infra tempus compoti accidentes quo tempore hospicium domini erat apud Colyweston ultra ij septimanas mensis Septembris quibus erat ad custus hospicii domini forinseci et ultra unam septimanam mensis Octobris tempore paccacionis et ponderacionis lane domini in qua erat ad custus ipsius domini pro qualibet septimana xij^d prout habere consuevit, xxj^s. Et in consimilibus vadiis ipsius computantis per ij vices tempore vacacionis eiusdem
iiijs
hospicii existentis apud Whithall, prima vice per iiij^or septimanas inter xx diem Februarii et primum diem Aprilis tunc proximum ultra unam septimanam in qua erat ad mensam cum auditore domini, et secunda vice inter xxiiij diem Aprilis et primum diem Junii tunc proximum similiter infra tempus compoti per v septi-
vs
manas ad xij^d in septimanam ut supra, per quod tempus hospicium erat apud Whithall predictum etc. ix^s.

examinatur Summa iiij^li iij^s iiij^d.

[1] *Sic.*

Liberacio denariorum (Marg.)

Nota pro veteri ecclesia de Tattishall[1] (Marg.)

Et in denariis liberatis Willelmo Stanlowe Receptori domini generali ad manus Johannis Irlond Senescalli hospicii domini
xxs
Standardi ut in precio lx karffs turbarum emptarum ad Swyneshed
iiijs
Fenn'. cariagio earundem de ibidem usque fossatum iuxta cimiterium ecclesie de Tateshale per aquam mense Januarii infra tempus compoti
xs viijd
mensa et regardo ij hominum de Wymondham in comitatu Norffolk existentium apud Tateshale super facturam fagottorum in bosco domini vocato Ffrithkarhage pro eodem hospicio mensibus Februarii
xs
et Marcii, stipendio diversorum hominum colligencium lx. carectas
xxs
focalis sicci in bosco de Myntyng carecta ad ij^{d} cum cariagio eiusdem de ibidem, usque Tupholme dyke per carectas et de ibidem usque
xixs
Tateshale per aquam.

sicut xlix^{s} *pro collectione et cariagio lx carectatarum scicci*[2] *focalis in sua propria allocacione et non ad onus dicti Senescalli hospicii etc.* (Marg.)

Stipendio Johannis Drawall et socii sui cariancium xxx quarteria
ijd
brasii de Braunceton usque Tateshale, eiusdem cariancis xxv
ijs
quarteria aveni de Boston[2] usque Tateshale super expensis

[membrane 2]
vjd
eiusdem hospicii mense Novembris . succ' focale in Chacea de Tateshale pro carbone inde fiendo pro eodem hospicio, ac cum
viijs viijd
denariis solutis Johanni Kent pro factura et combustione eiusdem focalis per xxvj dies mensibus Octobris et Novembris, factura
iiijli vjs viijd
et cariagio de vj^{ml} cccc . $iiij^{x}$ x fagottorum de Frithkarr'hagge super expensis dicti hospicii domini Standardi M^{l} ad $xiij^{s}$ $iiij^{d}$ in toto per parcellas predictas. ix^{li} iij^{s} vj^{d}.

Et in denariis liberatis eidem Receptori ad manus Petri (Idle)[1]
xxd
Senescalli hospicii domini forinseci ut in factura et cariagio ccc brueriarum factarum in parco de Tateshale mense Augusti erga
iijs viijd
adventum domini ibidem. Stipendio Johannis Drawall per xj dies mensibus Augusti et Septembris cariantis cum batella panem et cervisiam de Boston usque Tateshale super expensis eiusdem hospicii
iiijs
ad $iiij^{d}$ per diem ac cum factura et cariagio ccc fagottorum vocatorum

[1] This is in a later hand, probably early sixteenth century. [2] *Sic*.

ellerkiddes de copicia predicta apud Frithkarr' super expensis dicti hospicij in toto per parcellas predictas testatur etc. lix^{s} $iiij^{d}$.

Respondet Willelmus Stanlowe generalis Receptor in compoto suo huius anni de ista summa.

Summa ix^{li} xij^{s} x^{d}.

SUMMA OMNIUM ALLOCACIONUM ET LIBERACIONUM CCCC. LIX^{li} IX^{s} X^{d} OB'.

ET HABET SUPERPLUSAGIUM $CXVJ^{li}$ IX^{s} J^{d} OB.

Et ulterius allocatur ei ix^{s} vj^{d} pro factura M^{l} $iiij^{c}$ $iiij^{xx}$ x fagottorum in copicio predicto vocato Frithkarr mense Aprilis anni precedentis super expensis hospicii domini Standardi de tempore Gilberti Knaresburgh' tunc custodis eiusdem qualibet centena ad $viij^{d}$.

ET SIC HABET SUPERPLUSAGIUM $CXVJ^{li}$ $XVIIJ^{s}$ VIJ^{d} OB.

Et respectuantur ei xv^{s} de precio iij^{ml} tegularum venditarum Johanni Weende in anno precedente quas dicit dominum sibi perdonasse. Igitur in respectu quousque loquitur cum domino.

iiijs iiijd

Et eidem lxxv^{s} x^{d} de feodo ipsius Thome Croxby pro anno integro

xxiijs vjd

finiente in Festo Pasche anno xvj^{mo} predicto, et Ricardi Sawer pro iii quarteriis anni iuxta afferenciam xxx^{s} per annum in respectu ex mandato domini quousque etc.[1]

SUMMA RESPECTUATIONUM $IIIJ^{li}$ X^{s} X^{d}

Et super (Marg.)

Rogerum Barker ballivum domini apud Boston in precio vj chaldirs carbonum maritimorum quos dicit se liberasse pro expensis thoralis calcini dicti castri quorum tamen recepcionem iste idem computans denegat. Igitur super ipsum Rogerum iterum positum. Sunt prec' le[1] chaldir v^{s}. xxx^{s}.

[*Dorse*]

COMPOTUS THOME CROXBY

Summa allocationum respectuationum et unde super $cccclxvj^{li}$ ij^{d} ob'. Quibus allocatis et deductis constat ipsum esse in superplusagio $cxxij^{li}$ xix^{s} v^{d} ob'. De qua quidem summa recepit de exitu domorum domini in comitatu Lincoln' post determinacionem compotorum ibidem ad Festum Sancti Michaelis anno $xvij^{mo}$ predicto per parcellas inferius annotatas lj^{li} ix^{s} v^{d}. Et quibus sic deductis est adhuc in superplusagio $lxxj^{li}$ x^{s} ob'. Pro qua quidem [s]umma ostendit nomina creditorum extendencium ad summam. $iiij^{xx}j^{li}$ xv^{s} x^{d}.

[1] *Sic.*

NOMINA CREDITORUM.[1]

quia iste computans in anno proximo subsequente iterum computavit et . . . tam isti creditores quam alii particulariter annotatur (Marg.)

Johannes Mason xxiiij^{s}
Robertus Mason xiij^{s} iiij^{d}
Godfridus Brekmason xl^{s}
Matheus Brekmason xl^{s}
Jacobus Brekmason xxxvij^{s}
Cristinus Brekmason xliij^{s}
Johannes Ramsey xx^{s}
Johannes Warner xxvj^{s} viij^{d}
Willelmus Pepir xx^{s}
Ricardus Grebby x^{s}
Johannes Sleght xxiiij^{s}
Thomas Botiller vij^{s} ii^{d}
Willelmus Loode vj^{s} vj^{d}
Willelmus Danby iij^{s} iiij^{d}
Thomas Toly ii^{s}
Johannes Perche vij^{s} vj^{d}
Willelmus Sawer xxxv^{s}
Johannes Chambour iiij^{s}
Johannes Freston iij^{s}
Willelmus Peccham iij^{s} iiij^{d}
Johannes Bonour xxxiij^{s} x^{d}
Johannes Thomson xviij^{s}
Edmundus Ussher xx^{s}

Johannes Loksmyth liij^{s} iiij^{d}
Radulphus Smyth xxxij^{s}
Johannes Drawall xviij^{d}
Robertus Clerk viij^{s}
Willelmus Borell xvj^{s}
Johannes Swyne x^{s} viij^{d}
Johannes Prentys viij^{s} viij^{d}
Johannes Flixburn xxv^{s} vij^{d}
Henricus Plummer vij^{s} ij^{d}
Persona de Ingoldmelles xlvj^{s} viij^{d}
Johannes Kighley xx^{s}
Johannes Sawer xxij^{s}
Willelmus Levely xxxv^{s} x^{d}
Abbas de Kirkstede vj^{s} viij^{d}
Johannes Hert lxxiij^{s} iiij^{d}
Johannes Betson xxviij^{li} xvj^{s}
Ricardus Palmer iij^{s}
Ricardus Swyne lxvj^{s} viij^{d}
Johannes Borell lxvj^{s} viij^{d}
Robertus Trewlofe iiij^{s} iiij^{d}
Thomas Tumby xx^{d}
Robertus Tyler vj^{s}
Foys Brekemaker iiij^{s} iiij^{d}
Johannes Lowys iiij^{li} viij^{s} j^{d}
Johannes Docheman x^{s}
iiij^{xx}j^{li} xv^{s} x^{d}

[At other head of dorse.]

. . . . *maioris* (Marg.)

Idem respondit de cc^{m}xlvij^{ml} ix^{c} tegulis maioris forme receptis de remanentia anni precedentis. Et de iiij^{c}iiij^{xx}x^{ml}vij^{c} tegulis huius forme factis hoc anno ut infra per Foys Brekmaker ad equivalenciam precii. Et de viij^{ml} ix^{c} tegulis huius forme emptis hoc anno ut infra de Johanne Chamberleyn firmario thoralis domini apud Boston hoc anno tam de arreragiis quam exitu firme sue.

Summa vij^{cm} xlvij^{ml}D.

De quibus computat fore operatum super muracione de le Countre mure infra Castrum de Tateshale operata per Matheum Brekman et socios suos ut infra ciiij^{xx}ij^{ml}. Et expenduntur super nova edificacione unius magni stabuli infra castrum ad finem occidentalem de le Wolhous per Godfridum Brekman et socios suos infra tempus

[1] The whole of this list has been cancelled by a large cross drawn through it.

compoti ut infra ccxxxvj^{ml}. Et expenduntur in fundamento unius parve domus inter ipsum stabulum et le Wolhous operato per dictum Godfridum Brekman et socios suos ut infra . xlvj^{ml}. Et in vendicione ut infra Rogero Preestes de Hornecastr' de tegulis domini in Edlyngton mora M^{l}Dcc. Et expenduntur in opere cementario molendinarum domini apud Tateshale xxv^{ml}. Et dantur ex elemosina domini super operibus fabrice ecclesie de Edlyngton M^{l}M^{l}M^{l}. Et expenduntur in diversis aliis operibus infra idem castrum ut in refeccionibus parietum caminorum parietum domus mercati operatis per dietam et non per millenam, per estimacionem per easdem dietas c xiiij^{ml}. Et expenduntur in caminis et fenestris dicti stabuli de tegulis operatis vocatis hewentile M^{l}M^{l}cc^{ml}. Summa DCIX^{ml} DCCCC.

Et remanent cxxxvij^{ml}vj^{cm} unde in disposicione Baldewyni Brekman de totis tegulis deficientibus ad thorale de parte tegularum ibidem annotatarum fore remanentium anno precedente cxxxiiij^{ml} DC et infra castrum iij^{ml}.

Fagotti (Marg.)

Et de xv^{ml}cc^{ma}lx fagottis hoc anno sucscisis[1] in bosco domini vocato Stikeswold Southwod' pro expensis thoralis domini apud Edlyngton more ut infra. Summa xv^{ml}cc^{m}lx.

De quibus in decima data Priorisse de Stikeswold pro fagottis succisis hoc anno ut supra M^{l}Dxxx. Et in vendicione ut infra super expensis thoralis domini predicti pro combustione tegularum ex recognicione et sacramento computantis xiij^{ml}vij^{cma}xxx.
examinatur. Summa que supra Et equet.

III

Welby, 29 September, 1438—29 September 1439.

Liberaciones denariorum

Et eidem Receptori ad manus Thome Croxby Clerici operum Castri
lxiiij*s* vij*d*
de Tateshale super empcione petrarum liberarum pro operibus eiusdem Castri per parcellas in billa ipsius computantis super hunc
xiiij*s* x*d*
computum liberata testatas, et cariagio earundem de ibidem querrie usque Appiltrenesse per consimiles parcellas ibidem testatas.

lxxxviij^{s} v^{d}

Et eidem Receptori ad manus prefati Thome Croxby super cariagio xxxv carectarum plastri Parrisiensis de Londonthorp usque Appeltrenesse super operibus Castri de Tateshale ad diversas vices infra tempus compoti accidentis.

xlj^{s}

[1] *Sic.*

IV

31 May, 1439—27th March, 1440.

Officium Supervisoris operum Castri de Tateshale (Marg.)

COMPOTUS THOME CROXBY SUPERVISORIS OPERUM RADULPHI DOMINI CROMWELL C[ASTRI] SUI DE TATESHALE PREDICTI AB ULTIMO DIE MAIJ ANNO REGNI REGIS HENRI SEXTI X . . . USQUE FESTUM PASCHE ACCIDENTEM XXVIJMO (DIE)[1] MARCII EX TUNC PROXIMO SEQUENTEM PER CCC^{m} DIES.

Arreragia (Marg.)

Idem respondet de vj^{li} x^{d} de arreragiis ultimi compoti anni proximi precedentis prout patet in pede ibidem.

Summa vj^{li} x^{d}

Recepta denariorum de Generali Receptore domini (Marg.)

Et de cccliij^{li} xx^{d} obolo quadrante receptis de Willelmo Stanlowe Receptore domini Generali per manus diversorum ministrorum [in] comitatu Lyncoln' super operibus castri predicti per tempus huius compoti prout tam in compoto ipsius Generalis Receptoris quam in compotis eorund[em] ministrorum terminatis ad festum Sancti Michaelis anno Regis nunc xviij^{mo} particulariter continetur. Et de lxxv^{s} receptis de ..... Receptore domini Generali per manus Roberti Gowshill clerici Receptoris domini in comitatibus Not' Derb' et Leycestr' ut in precio xxv carectat [arum plastre] Parisiensis provenientis de exitu dominii de Granby et venditi isti computanti super operibus predictis prout in compoto ipsius Receptoris in titulo ...... denar' plene liquet.

Summa ccclvj^{li} xvj^{s} viiij^{d} obolus quadrans

Vendicio tegularum fagottorum et turbarum (Marg.)

Et de xij^{s} vj^{d} de precio M^{l}M^{l}D tegularum maioris forme vocatarum waltyle venditarum diversis personis hoc anno ut ..... precio millene . v^{s}. Et precio fagottorum hoc anno expenditorum super clausura haiarum et combustione tegularum in thorali ut extra non respondit eo quod nulla vendicio fuerat de fagottis domini propriis set tamen provenientibus de empcione. Set respondit de liij^{s} iiij^{d} de precio lx carffs turbarum provenientium de parte illarum turbarum que empte fuerunt in Kesteven fenn' per ipsum computantem in anno precedente sic per ipsum co[mputantem] ... vendite Johanni Dokkynge de Whaplode ex eius noticia super compotum.

Summa xlv^{s} x^{d}

Vendicio ordij et veteris meremii (Marg.)

Et de xiiij^{li} vij^{s} de precio xxxvij quarteriorum v bussellorum ordii receptorum de granario domini per manus Ricardi Sawer cus[todis] eiusdem ut de huiusmodi grano proveniente de partibus

Norffolk ante festum Pasche infra tempus huius compoti ad diversa precia prout parcel[le] .... in libro parcellarum istius computantis huius anni annotantur. Et de lxvj^{s} viij^{d} receptis de Willelmo Plummer de Lyn ..... pro veteri meremio proveniente de j domo ibidem per dominum de ipso Willelmo empto sic sibi per ipsum computantem vendito.

Summa xvij^{li} xiij^{s} viij^{d}

Recepta de cofris domini (Marg.)

Et de vij^{li} receptis de cofris domini per manus diversorum videlicet Mathei Dyker tam per manus $^{xx s}$ Willelmi Stanlowe quam $^{lx s}$ Ricardi Westby ad ij vices. $^{xl s}$ Baldewyni Brekmaker et $^{xx s}$ Johannis Mason ex mera et propria recognicione ipsius computantis super hunc compotum. Et de vj^{li} xvij^{s} viij^{d} receptis de eisdem cofris domini per manus Radulphi Harple clerici Receptoris domini in comitatu Norffolk .... denar' solvent' ad manus Ricardi Flynt mense Marcii anno regis nunc xviij^{mo} predicto. Et de viij^{li} receptis de eis[dem] cofris domini ad manus eiusdem Ricardi Flynt pro tot denariis receptis in quadam baga ipsius Thome Croxby computan[tis] . post festum Purificacionis beate Marie Virginis anno xviij^{mo} predicto. Et de iiij^{li} ij^{s} vj^{d} ob'. receptis de eisdem cofris [domini] per manus Johannis Lowys de Boston apud Tateshale mense Marcii anno xviij^{mo} predicto.

Summa xxvj^{li} ij^{d} ob'.

Recepta de Johanne Weende (Marg.)

Et de iiij^{li} viij^{s} receptis de Johanne Weende super precium M^{l}M^{l}cc^{ma} faggottorum ab ipso Johanne Gedney et aliis emptorum apud Horsyngton pro expensis thoralis tegulini domini super Edelyngton more precio centene iiij^{s} prout in compoto ipsius Johannis Weende terminato in festo sancti Valentini proximo ante clausum huius compoti in titulo liberacionis denariorum plenius continetur.

Summa iiij^{li} viij^{s}

Oneratio novorum creditorum (Marg.)

Et de vj^{li} viij^{s} x^{d} receptis de Ricardo Flynt super solucione certorum creditorum huius officii quorum nomina cum eorum summis particularibus in compoto per ipsum Ricardum reddito simul cum hoc compoto et aliis compotis infilat'[1] ista remanente particulariter continentur. Et de liij^{li} viij^{s} de superonere novorum creditorum de toto tempore istius computantis tangentis officium clerici operum castri de Tateshale quorum nomina cum eorum summis extra separatim continentur.

Summa lix^{li} xvj^{s} x^{d}

SUMMA TOTALIS RECEPTE CUM ARRERAGIIS CCCCLXXIIJ^{li} IJ^{s} J^{d}

[1] *Sic.* What is intended is evidently *in filacia ista infilata*, as in another entry further on.

Superplusagium (Marg.)

De quibus computat in superplusagio ultimi compoti sui anni proximo precedentis prout patet in pede ibidem cxxij^{li} xix^{s} v^{d} ob.

Summa cxxij^{li} xix^{s} v^{d} ob.

Custus edificii Castri de Tateshale. (Marg.)

Et in diversis custibus misis et expensis factis ac appositis super operibus Castri de Tateshale per totum tempus huius compoti tam per ipsum computantem quam Ricardum Flynt sicut per parcellas in quodam quaterno papiri confecto super hunc compotum ostensas et particulariter examinatas ac inter memoranda eiusdem remanentes evidenter et particulariter continentur cum xlv^{li} xviij^{d} obolo solutis per ipsum Ricardum Flynt Auditorem domini inter festum Natalis domini anno xviij^{mo} predicto et festum Pasche extunc proxime sequentem in clausum huius compoti etc. cccxx^{li} x^{d}.

Summa cccxx^{li} x^{d}

Solucio firme manerii et grangie de Marton cum aliis (Marg.)

Et in denariis per predictum Ricardum Flynt solutis Priorisse de Staynefeld pro firma manerii et grangie de Marton in persolucionem eiusdem annis[1] finientibus in festo apostolorum Philipi et Jacobi anno Regis nunc xviij^{mo} per acquietantiam restitutam lxix^{s} v^{d} ob. Et in consimilibus denariis solutis per eundem Ricardum Flynt Johanni Howson de Conyngisby in parte solucionis xx^{s} eidem solutis pro ij parcellis prati ab eo emptis et inclusis infra quoddam novum clausum domini iuxta molendinum de Tateshale ultra xvj^{s} viij^{d} per eun[dem] Ricardum eidem Johanni solutis et allocatis in quodam ratiocinio facto per ipsum Ricardum inter festum Pasche anno xviij^{mo} predicto et festum nativitatis Sancti Johannis Baptiste extunc proximo sequentem . in filacia ista infilatur. iij^{s} iiij^{d}

Summa lxxij^{s} ix^{d} ob.

[membrane 2]

Liberacio forinseca (Marg.)

Et in denariis reliberatis Rogero Barker ballivo domini apud Boston ut in precio vj chaldrorum carbonum maritimorum quos dixit se liberasse super expensis thoralis calcini infra castrum predictum quarum quidem recepcionem iste computans denegat. Igitur super ipsum Rogerum reonerantur etc.[1] xxx^{s}.

Summa xxx^{s}

[2]Respondet Rogerus Barker ballivus de Boston in compoto suo ibidem tractato in festo sancti Michaelis anno Regis nunc xviij^{mo} in titulo *Recepta forinseca* ibidem.

Summa xxx^{s}[2]

SUMMA OMNIUM ALLOCACIONUM ET LIBERACIONUM—CCCCXLVIIJ^{li} IIJ^{s} J^{d}. ET DEBET XXIIIJ^{li} XIX^{s} QUADRANTEM.

[1] *Sic.*

[2-2] This entry is not part of the original account but is begun in the margin and written half across the membrane.

Et respectuatur ei xv^{s} de precio iij^{ml} tegularum venditarum Johanni Weende in anno secundo precedente, quas dicit dominum sibi perdonasse. Igitur in respectu quousque loquitur cum domino
iiij^{s} iiij^{d}
...... Et eidem—lxxv^{s} x^{d} de feodo ipsius Thome Croxby pro uno anno integro finiente in festo Pasche anno Regis nunc predicto
xxij...
xvj^{mo} et Ricardi Sawer pro tribus quartis anni iuxta afferenciam xxx^{s} per annum in respectu ex mandato domini quousque.[1] Et eidem xiij^{li} viij^{s} ix^{d} pro tot denarii[s] solutis Baldewyno Brekmaker super factura et anelacione tegularum in Edlyngton more vocatarum waltyle pro operibus infra castrum predictum ultra eas ut extra in dor[so] huius compoti specificatas super operibus castri predicti liberatas eo quod adhuc non liberantur. Igitur in respectu quousque liberentur etc.[1] Et eidem xxxix^{s} vij^{d} .... precio c^{ma}xx tabularum vocatarum weynscotes de parte ccc^{ma} huiusmodi tabularum emptarum apud Skegnesse per Johannem atte Hall juniorem ballivum de Candelesby super [oper]ibus castri de Tateshale ultra cv^{xx} de eisdem tabulis hoc anno liberatis super operibus predicti castri et inter parcellas edificiorum ibidem superius allocatis in respectu eo quod adhuc non liberantur set remanent apud Ingolmels in domo Thome Lowys ut asseritur per ipsum Johannem atte Hall tamen in respectu quousque etc.[1]

SUMMA RESPECTUATIONIS XIX^{li} XIX^{s} IJ^{d}. ET REMANENT ULTRA—.

Super —— ipsum Thomam Croxby computantem clare —— iiij^{li} xix^{s} x^{d} quadrans.

.. qua quidem summa iiij^{li} xix^{s} x^{d} quadrans idem Thomas computans oneratur superius in titulo *Recepta de coffro domini* cum viij^{li} receptis in bursa sua prout patet ibidem, quo quidem viij^{li} .. erunt de bonis propriis ipsius Thome ut supponitur.

[*Dorse*]

COMPOTUS THOME CROXBY

NOMINA CREDITORUM

Johannes Mason (viij^{s} viij^{d})^{c}
....*totum per Johannem Wende* (Marg.)

iij^{s} iiij^{d}
Robertus Thymelby mason (x^{s})^{c}
[*Inde*] *solutum vj^{s} viij^{d}* (Marg.)

Godefridus Brekmason xxx^{s}

Matheus Brekmason (xvij^{s} viij^{d})^{c}
....*totum per eundem Johannem* (Marg.)

Jacobus Brekmason xxxvj^{s} viij^{d}

[1] *Sic.*

Cristinus Brekmason *....totum per eundem Johannem* (Marg.)	(xxxvj^{s} viij^{d})^{c}
uxor Johannis Dauber [*In*]*de solutum vj^{s} viij^{d}* (Marg.)	*v^{s} iiij^{d}* (xij^{s})^{c}
Thomas Botiller	iij^{s} iiij^{d}
Johannes Perche *Inde solutum x^{s} ut supra* (Marg.)	*iij^{s} iiij^{d}* (xiij^{s} iij^{d})^{c}
Willelmus Sawer *Inde solutum xiij^{s} iiij^{d} ut supra* (Marg.)	*x^{s}* (xxiij^{s} iiij^{d})^{c}
Willelmus Grabye *Solutum totum* (Marg.)	(iiij^{s})^{c}
Johannes Loksmyth *Inde solutum xxxiij^{s} iiij^{d}* (Marg.)	*vj^{s} viij^{d}* (xl^{s})^{c}
Radulfus Smyth *Solutum totum* (Marg.)	(iiij^{s} ij^{d})^{c}
Robertus Clerk de Boston	viij^{s}
Johannes Hert	xl^{s}
Willelmus Borell'	iiij^{s}
Henricus Plommer	ij^{s}
Johannes Flixburn	ij^{s} vj^{d}
Johannes Betson *solutum totum per ipsum Johannem Wende* (Marg.)	(xxiiij^{li} xvij^{s} ij^{d})^{s}
Ricardus Swyne *Inde solutum vj^{s} viij^{d}* (Marg.)	*lx^{s}* (lxvj^{s} viij^{d})^{c}
Johannes Borell *Inde solutum xiij^{s} iiij^{d}* (Marg.)	*xxxiij^{s} iiij^{d}* (xlvj^{s} viij^{d})^{c}
Thomas Stoyle	vj^{s} viij^{d}
Johannes Roper *solutum totum ut supra* (Marg.)	(xij^{d})^{c}
Willemus Wodeson *solutum totum ut supra* (Marg.)	(xx^{s})^{c}
Agnes Besyngham de Kyme	iij^{s} iiij^{d}
Johannes Toynton	ij^{s} vj^{d}
Willelmus Peccham	iij^{s}
Johannes Swyne *solutum totum* (Marg.)	(iiij^{s} viij^{d})^{c}

	xj*s*
Johannes Bonour	(xvij^{s} viij^{d})^{c}
Inde solutum vj^{s} viij^{d} ut supra (Marg.)	
Willelmus Rokerey	xx^{d}
Solutum totum (Marg.)	
Willelmus Levely	iij^{s}
Johannes Lowys	xxiiij^{s}
Willelmus Holwel	(xvj^{d})^{c}
Solutum totum (Marg.)	
Willelmus Fissher	(xxiij^{s} iiij^{d})^{c}
Solutum totum (Marg.)	
Willelmus Ablet	iiij^{s}
Abbas de Kirkstede	(xxx^{s})^{c}
Solutum totum (Marg.)	
	xx*d*
Johannes Chambr'	(v^{s})^{c}
Inde solutum iij^{s} iiij^{d} (Marg.)	

LIIJ^{li} VIIJ^{s} (Marg.)

[*At other head of dorse*]

[TEG]ULE

Infrascriptus computans respondit de cxxxvij^{ml}dc tegulis maioris forme receptis de remanentia anni precedentis. Et de cccc^{ml}xxiiij^{ml}d tegulis factis hoc anno per Baldewynum Brekmaker ad equivalenciam precii. Et de xxiij^{ml} tegulis huius forme emptis hoc anno ut infra de Johanne Chamberleyn firmario thoralis domini apud Boston tam de arreragiis quam de exitu firme sue huius anni.

Summa DCXXXVJ^{ml}C.

De quibus computat fore operatum super le pavyng magni stabuli et edificacione de lez ponyons eiusdem ad ij vices tam per dietas quam per millenas ex testimonio carectariorum xxviij^{ml}d. Et expenduntur super novo edificione parietum unius domus scituate[1] inter stabulum et domum molendini tam per dietas quam per millenas ex huiusmodi testimonio super hunc compotum—xlviij^{ml}dc. Et expenduntur in diversis aliis operibus domini infra castrum predictum ut in refeccionibus parietum exaltacione de le ij galeryes ac eciam parietum castri ad finem coquine et caminorum et alias in pluribus operibus operatis per dietas tamen prout tam estimantur per huiusmodi dietas quam testimonium et sacramentum predictorum

xx M1

carectariorum—ciiij xv^{ml}. ix^{c}. Et in vendicione ut infra Edmundo

M1D

Ussher et Thome Rudde de tegulis domini super Edlyngton more

[1] *Sic.*

M^{l}M^{l}D. Et dantur Abbati de Kirkestede ex mandato domini hoc anno v^{ml}.

Summa cciiij$^{xx ml}$ D	Et remanent ccclv^{ml} unde in disposicione Baldewyni Brekmaker cxxxiiij^{ml}dc^{ml} et super novum fossatum iuxta castrum ccxxj^{ml}.

Fagotta (Marg.)

Et de ix^{ml} faggottis receptis de empcione hoc anno ut infra de Abbate de Kirkestede tam apud$^{iiij^{ml}}$ Braken' quam Highawe$^{v^{ml}}$ ex noticia computantis. Et de M^{l}M^{l}cc^{ma} receptis de empcione hoc anno similiter ut infra de feoffatoribus Willelmi Ratheby. Et de viij^{cma} iiij^{xx} huiusmodi faggottis receptis similiter de empcione hoc anno ut infra apud Thorneton Wood. Et de iiij^{cma} fagottis receptis de empcione de vicario de Stixwold hoc anno ut infra.

Summa xij^{ml}iiij^{c}iiij^{xx}

De quibus expenduntur in sepacionibus circa magnum clausum inter Snawdon et Kirkestede v^{ml}. Et expenduntur in combustione thoralis domini apud Edlyngton more ex recognicione et sacramento computantis, vij^{ml} iiij^{c} iiij^{xx}.

Summa que supra. Et eque.

V

25th March, 1445—25th March, 1446.

Officium Clerici operum Dominii de Tateshale (Marg.)

Compotus Johannis Southell Clerici operum Domini Cromwell Castri et dominii sui de Tateshale a festo Annunciationis Dominice anno regni regis Henrici sexti xxiij^{cio} usque idem festum Annunciationis beate Marie extunc proximo sequens anno eiusdem regis xxiij^{to} per unum annum integrum.

Arreragia (Marg.)

Idem reddidit compotum de xxv^{li} viij^{s} ij^{d} de arreragiis ultimi compoti sui anni proximi precedentis prout patet in pede ibidem.

Summa xxv^{li} viij^{s} ij^{d}

Recepta de denariis Receptoris domini (Marg.)

Et de ccccxl^{li} iiij^{s} iiij^{d} receptis de Roberto Wymbissh clerico Receptori Domini in Comitatu Lyncoln' ut de exitu officii sui de anno finiente in festo sancti Michaelis anno predicti Regis nunc xxiiij^{to} prout in compoto ipsius Roberti inde reddito plenius continetur. Et de xxvij^{s} vj^{d} receptis de Henrico Etwall Receptori Domini in Comitatibus Nottingham Derby Leycestr' et Stafford de exitu dominii de Typshelff super cariagio plumbi de Pecco usque Lyncoln prout in compoto suo ibidem plenius continetur.

Summa ccccxlj^{li} xj^{s} x^{d}

Vendiciones forinsece (Marg).

Et de l^{s} v^{d} de precio unius pipe vini rubei veteris vendite per ipsum computantem extra celarium domini ex eius mandato mense Maii infra tempus huius compoti ex noticia sua super hunc compotum. Et de xj^{s} de precio j stethy[1] ferri de veteri remanente domini sic venditi Radulpho Smyth per ipsum computantem hoc anno. Et de x^{s} de precio M^{l}M^{l} tegularum maioris forme venditarum Gardiano ecclesie Collegiate de Tateshale hoc anno ut extra.

Summa lxxj^{s} v^{d}

SUMMA TOTIUS RECEPTE CUM ARRERAGIIS CCCCLXX^{li} XJ^{s} V^{d}

Allocatio superplusagii (Marg.)

De quibus computat in allocatione superplusagii ultimi compoti sui anni proximo precedentis prout patet in pede ibidem lij^{s} viij^{d}.

Summa lij^{s} viij^{d}

Custus edificiorum (Marg.)

Et in custibus novi edificii fossati plantacionis ac divisorum aliorum edificiorum et operum factorum infra Castrum de Tateshale ac

[1] *Sic.*

lli vijd
Whithall et alibi per predictum tempus huius compoti ut in stipendio
lathomorum liberorum operancium in diversis operibus suis cemen-
lxxiijli xijs ixd
tariorum vocatorum Brekmasons similiter operancium in diversis
xxxviijli xijs xjd
operibus suis ibidem. Carpentariorum consimili modo operancium
xxxli xijs iijd
in diversis operibus suis. Emptione petrarum liberarum cum cariagio.
iiijxx vjli xs vjd
Custu thoralis tegulini cum empcione focalis super combustura
tegularum et cum cariagio earundem tam per terram quam per
lxli xvijs ijd
aquam. Stipendio laborariorum laborancium in diversis operibus
vjli vs xid ob.
suis. Cariagio meremii fagotorum lapidum et carbonum per aquam.
xli xs xjd
Stipendio sarratorum cum eorum operibus ad diversas vices. Custu
xvli viijs xjd ob.
thoralis calcini cum empcione carbonum et focalis pro eodem.
vjli xixs viijd ob. vjli xiijs iiijd
Empcione necessariorum pro operibus. Custu fossati et sepacionis.
xliijli viijs ijd
Empcione ferramentorum cum fabricacione eorundem. Empcione
xiijli
petrarum liberarum vocatarum sandstones tam pro edificiis apud
cvijs vjd
Whithall et Burwell quam pro stagno vocato le Syncarr. Stipendio
plumbatorum cum cariagio plumbi de Pecco usque Tateshale.
vjli xvijs viijli vjs xd
Empcione cordarum pro operibus. Empcione plastri Parisiensis
iiijli xijs iijd
cum cariagio et operacione. Emendacione arcuum sagittarum cum
xlijs jd
mundacione alii harnesii infra castrum. Custu volucionis lane et
cvijs iiijd ob.
aliorum infra lanariam. Mensa ipsius computantis cum feodo et mensa Roberti Tyler per tempus huius compoti prout plenius et particulariter apparet in uno quaterno papiri inde confecto super hunc compotum liberato et in baga compotorum huius anni remanente.—ccccxlvj^{li} vj^{s} iij^{d}

Summa ccccxlvj^{li} vj^{s} iij^{d}

SUMMA OMNIUM ALLOCATIONUM PREDICTARUM—CCCXLVIIJ^{li} XVIIJ^{s} XJ^{d}

ET DEBET XXJ^{li} XIJ^{s} VJ^{d}

Unde respectuatur ei : (Marg.)

xv^{li} pro feodo suo causa istius eiusdem officii sui pro iiij^{or} annis dimidio finientibus in festo Pasche anno Regis nunc xxiij^{to} per annum lxvj^{s} viij^{d} prout secum concordatum est ut dicit. Et eidem—xj^{li} xvj^{s} viij^{d} de denariis solutis Baldewyno Brekemaker super factura et anelacione tegularum in Edlyngton more vocatorum waltile pro operibus infra castrum predictum ultra certas tegulas in dorso huius compoti specificatas super operibus castri predicti liberatas eo quod adhuc non liberantur.

SUMMA RESPECTUATIONIS XXVJ^{li} XVJ^{s} VIIJ^{d}. Quibus, qui onerantur in compoto anni subsequentis in titulo *Arreragia.*

Quibus una cum misis predictis de totali
summa oneris deductis constat ipsum
computantem esse in superplusagio de—
allocatione in compoto anni subsequentis
ciiij^{s} ij^{d} pro quibus onerdit[1] nomina creditorum extendencium ad summam cxiiij^{s} ij^{d} ut inferius.

NOMINA CREDITORUM (Marg.)

Petrus Martyn iij^{s} x^{d}	Phineas Blynkasope xxj^{s}
Thomas Ratheby ij^{s} x^{d} ob.	Johannes Conns ij^{s} ij^{d}
Petrus Dyker xiij^{s} iiij^{d}	Johannes Hert xiij^{s} iiij^{d}
Thomas Plommer v^{s}	Johannes Enterpath ix^{s} vij^{d}
John Cowper vj^{s} viij^{d}	Thomas Godefray } xxijs
Willelmus Ablot xiiij^{s}	Thomas Lauerans } iiij^{d} ob.

CXIIIJ^{s} IJ^{d} (Marg.)

[*Dorse*]

Tateshale (Marg.)

Compotus Johannis Southill clerici operum Castri de Tateshale terminatus ad festum Annunciationis dominice anno regni regis Henrici vj^{ti} xxiiij^{to}.

Anno xxiiij^{to}.

Tegule (Marg.)

Infrascriptus Baldewynus Brickmaker de cclxxiiij^{ml} tegulis receptis de remanentia anni precedentis. Et de ccciiij^{xx} iij^{ml} tegulis maioris forme factis hoc anno per eundem Baldewynum ad equevalenciam precii liberatis super operibus castri et reparacione tenementorum domini in Tateshale et alio modo per tempus compoti. Et de iiij^{xx} iiij^{ml} tegulis minoris forme factis per eundem Baldewynum et liberatis hoc anno ut supra.

Summa DCCXLI^{ml} DC^{m}

De quibus computat fore operata in magno turre vocato le Dongeon et aliis minutis operibus Castri de tegulis maioris forme per talliam ccc^{m} xxij^{ml}. Et expenditur super facture unius novi contremure facti ex avisamento domini in capite de le Syncarr de tegulis maioris forme similiter per tallium iiij^{xx} xiiij^{ml}. Et venduntur ut infra Gardiano ecclesie Collegiate de Tateshale pro nova factura unius domus infra tenementum in quo Johannes Warner manet de tegulis

[1] *Sic*: the letters *di* are plain where one would expect *a*: probably *recte onerat.*

maioris forme $M^{l}M^{l}$. Et dantur per dominum preposito ecclesie de Edlyngton super novo edificio eiusdem ecclesie de tegulis maioris forme v^{ml}.

Summa $ccccxxiij^{ml}$ { Et remanent ccc $xviij^{ml}$ DC^{m} unde c^{ml} super ripam novi fossati de tegulis $iiij^{xx}$ $iiij^{ml}$ maioris forme et minoris forme $ciiij^{xx}$ $iiij^{ml}$ et in manibus ipsius Baldewyni de antiquis arreragiis suis, $cxxxiiij^{ml}dc^{m}$

VI

Account for the year ending 29th September 1472.[1]

Tateshale (Marg.)

. . . compoti Ricardi Parker ballivi coll' redd' ac vendit' bosc' de anno integre finiente ad festum Sancti Michaelis Archangeli anno regni regis Edwardi iiij^{ti} xij^{mo}. . . . .

Reparacio facta infra Castellum ibidem.

Et solutum Henrico Dente carpentario pro factura de duobus novis pontibus ibidem operantibus seipso et duobus hominibus eius pro iiij^{xx} diebus particulariter capientibus per diem xvj^{d} . . . . . cvj

Et solutum Thome Sawer et socio suo pro carracione meiremii ibidem per convencionem in gross. . . x^{s}

Et solutum Thome Colynson laborer pro auxiliacione carpentariorum et fossacione ibidem operanti per xij dies capienti per diem iiij^{d} . . . .

Et solutum Willelmo Colynson pro consimili operacione operanti ibidem per xv dies per diem iiij d . . . .

Et solutum Johanni Smyth laborer pro consimili operanti ibidem per iiij dies per diem iiij^{d} . . . .

Et solutum Ricardo Graybe et Johanni Rayburne pro cariagio de xxxiij carettarum meiremii de Grubholme usque castrum capiente ad plaustrum iij^{d} . . . .

Et solutum Thome Caton et Ricardo Graybe pro cariagio de xiiij carrettarum meiremij de parco usque castrum predictum capientibus ad carrettam iiij^{d} . . . .

Liberaciones ad hospicium. (Marg.)

Et solutum Willelmo Smyth pro factura de V^{xx} et x de grossis clavis pro magno ponte iuxta stabulos[2] domini exteriores . . .

Et solutum Henrico Dente carpentario pro emendacione molendinario equino . . . .

Et solutum predictis Henrico et Johanni Wode Milner pro cogges et spyndillis pro predicto molendino equino emptis . . .

Et solutum Willelmo Horner tyler pro emendacione caminorum in coquinis iij^{s} . . . .

Et solutum dicto Willelmo Horner pro emendacione de le Ovenherth in le Bakhous—xxij . . . . .

Et solutum pro cariagio de ij carrettarum luti pro eadem reparacione facienda . . . .

Et solutum Thome Nevyle tyler operanti infra Castellum per xij dies . . . . . .

[1] This consists of eight paper sheets dealing with other matters than building operations. The heading is given but the sections preceding those dealing with the castle are omitted.

[2] *Sic.*

Et solutum dicto Thome Nevyle pro desursum capiend' tegularum apud turrum[1] super moram operanti ibidem per v dies capienti per diem die vj^{d} ....

Et solutum pro j bunnchet stonlatt' empto de Ricardo Leverton ......

Et solutum pro viij rygtyles emptis ......

Et solutum pro iij quarteriis et j bussello calcis emptis precio quartarii xij^{d} ......

Et solutum Willelmo Kelsey pro j whelebarowe pro habendo in castro ......

Summa ix^{li} vij^{s} vj^{d}

[1] *Sic.*

Translation

I

15th February, 1434—2nd May, 1435

THE ACCOUNT OF THOMAS CROXBY, SUPERVISOR OF THE WORKS OF RALPH, LORD CROMWELL AT HIS CASTLE OF TATESHALE . . . IN SEPARATE SUMS OF MONEY RECEIVED BY HIM, AND LAID OUT BY HIM IN PAYMENTS AND EXPENSES FROM THE 15TH DAY OF FEBRUARY IN THE 12TH YEAR OF THE REIGN . . . UNTIL THE 2ND DAY OF MAY IN THE 13TH YEAR OF THE SAME KING.

Arrears

None because there was a surplus in the last account.

Receipts of money from the issues of the office of the Receiver-General.

But the same[1] accounts for moneys received from the issues of the office of William Stanlowe, receiver-general of my lord, by the hands of various bailiffs, in moneys to be laid out upon the work of the aforesaid Castle during the time of the account, as detailed more particularly both in the account of the receiver-general himself and in those of the same bailiffs, terminating at Michaelmas, in the 13th year aforesaid and he acknowledges the receipt. £47-8s.-3d.

From Gilbert Knaresburgh.

For[2] the receipts of such moneys from Gilbert Knaresburgh, as part of his receipt from the coffer of my lord during the period of the account, as particularly appears from two bills on account, which have been shown and are among the items remaining to be recorded in this account, of which the first, dated 14th March in the 12th year, contains £133-0s.-9d. and the second, dated 1st May in the 13th year, contains £74-4s.-1d. £207-4s.-10d.

From Robert Gowshill, clerk.

For the receipts of such moneys from Robert Gowshill, clerk, my lord's receiver in the shires of Nottingham, Derby and Leicester, from the issues of his receipts as for the year ending at

[1] I.e. Thomas Croxby.
[2] "He accounts" should be understood in each entry.

Michaelmas in the 13th year, by two indented bills,[1] remaining as above, of which the first, beginning 25th February in the 12th year, contains £79-16s.-11d., and the second, beginning 30th January in the 13th year, contains £12-6s.-8d. together with 100 shillings from the same accountant delivered to him without a bill. £117-3s.-7d.

From the sale of 4 *gaddes of Spanish iron.*

He acknowledges the price of 4 gaddes[2] of Spanish iron from the remainder in my lord's stock of that used in the preceding year during the period of the account on the works of the said castle, weight 314 lbs., price 5s.-6d. per 100 lbs., reckoned at the price of this kind of iron bought at the same time at Boston. 17s.-2d.

From the sale of wood and bark from Stikeswold south wode[3] and others of my lord's woods.

He acknowledges the price of 15,124 faggots, from the wood and underwood cut in my lord's wood called Stikeswold southwode, for firing bricks in my lord's brick kiln there ; price for each 1,000, over and above cutting, 23s.-4d., besides 1696 faggots assigned to the Prioress of Stikeswold in name of tithe.[4] £17-12s.-0d.

Price of bark from the oakwood of the aforesaid wood and underwood, sold in gross to Robert Fysshe, amounting to 6 cartloads, price of each load 2s. 12s.-0d.

Price of 74 cartloads of fuel, felled during the period of the account in Tateshale chase for burning in 10 limekilns for the said works, to each kiln 7½ cartloads, less in all one half cartload, the whole cost of the said carting (price of each cartload in accordance with the aforesaid preceding account being 12d.) amounting to £3-14s.-0d.

Price of 1 acre of wood and underwood bought out of my lord's coffer from the Abbot of Bardney[5]

[1] This of course is literally meant. The two copies of the bill were written out on a single sheet and then separated by a zig-zag cutting so that the indentations could be fitted together for future verification.

[2] A *gaddum* was a measure of iron. From the present entry it would appear that each *gaddum* weighed 78½ lb.

[3] Stixwould, about 8 miles N.W. of Tattershall. Of its Cistercian nunnery, referred to subsequently in the account, nothing now remains.

[4] There is a similar entry as to tithes of wood in the Kirby Muxloe building accounts (*Trans. Leicester Archæol. Soc.*, vol. XI, p. 336).

[5] The Benedictine abbey of Bardney was situated about 11 miles N.E. of Tattershall, between Lincoln and Horncastle. Little trace of it remains.

in the wood of Bardney in the month of March in the 12th year for the aforesaid works, for the cost of which, and for felling 130 small oaks, valuation was made and estimated according to the value of the adjoining acres amounting to £4-6s.-8d.

Price of 2½ acres of the same kind of wood and underwood bought from John Hert in the wood of the said Abbot of Bardney and paid from the said coffers of my lord in the month of March of the 13th year; price £4-6s.-8d. the acre, together with 15s. paid from the said coffers for the felling of the said wood at 6s. the acre. £11-11s.-8d.

Price of 17 small oaks from the issues of my lord's coppice in Tateshale chase called Thorpe Sheterley[1] for the aforesaid works, price of each 2d. 2s.-10d.

Price of 600 faggots out of 1,600 from the cropping and pruning of wood in the said acres of wood bought from the Abbot of Bardney as above, price of each 100 5s., besides 1,000 of these faggots carried to Tateshale for the said works.[2] £1-10s.-0d.

For the purchase of Waynscotts by my Lord at Hull.

Price of 200 boards called waynscotts obtained at Hull by my lord's provision from his own coffers, and thereafter sent in the month of February in the 12th year to Torkesey,[3] and thence to Tateshale for the works there, price of each 7d. £7-0s.-0d.[4]

Receipts for the board of workmen in my lord's household.

Sums received from John Crakehall, late warden of my lord's household, for the board of craftsmen and labourers[5] engaged on the works of the said castle between 15th February of the 12th year and the morrow of Michaelmas next thereafter, as it set forth more fully in the account of said former warden finishing on the said morrow of Michaelmas. £18-3s.-8d.

[1] Is this Tattershall Thorpe ?

[2] A marginal entry here notes £39 9s. 11d.

[3] These wainscots, doubtless "Eastland boards" evidently came by water, up the Trent to Torksey and thence by the Fossdyke to Lincoln, and from there by the Witham to Tattershall.

[4] Note that the reckoning is by "long hundreds"—i.e., 100 = 120.

[5] *Operariorum et laboriorum.* Note the distinction: *opus* and *operabilia* are regularly used in medieval Latin to signify handicrafts, i.e. skilled work, as distinct from *labor*, unskilled labour.

He will account next year.

For the board of the said workmen living in the foresaid household between the said Michaelmas and the 2nd May, not received in the closed account, because the books of the said household had not been audited. Therefore carried forward. *nil*

Default of creditors.

Sums in default : over the payment to Baldwin Brekeman (£10) for the making of bricks called waltile,[1] by reason of their being insufficiently kneaded, also the sum of £2-10s-6d. deducted from the carriage of sand both in the present and in the preceding year, because by agreement he is to bear the cost of such carriage ; and also in respect of sums discharged by him for leave not to reckon in the laying down, lifting and stacking of 600,000 bricks made this year, after their firing, at the rate of 1d. per 1,000, in accordance with the agreement made by John Fulnetby[2] and W. Stanlowe. £15-0s.-6d.

SUM OF THE WHOLE RECEIPTS £432-7s.-11d.

Allocation of surplus from the preceding account.

He reckons in the surplus from his last account, finishing 15th February in the 12th year of the present King, as is shown at the foot thereof. £11-12s.-4½d.

BUILDING EXPENSES AT TATTERSHALL CASTLE

Various outgoings and expenses incurred in the works of the said castle during the time of the account, as is particularly set forth in a certain sheet of paper made up in respect thereof, submitted and examined for accounting purposes, and entered among the items to be noted in the present account.

Purchase of stones.

£3-13s-4d. for the purchase of 560 free stones, 300 stones brought from the quarry of Willesford,[3] 160 stones from the quarry of Hesilburgh,[4] and 100 from the quarry of Skowpe,[5] price 13s.-4d.

[1] "Wall tile," i.e. bricks, as distinct from "thack-tile", roofing tiles.

[2] John may have been from Fulnetby, 8 miles N.E. of Lincoln or perhaps Fulletby in Hill Wapentake.

[3] Wilsford, some 4½ miles S.E. of Sleaford, or about 15 miles in the same direction from Tattershall. There was a Benedictine priory here. It was no doubt from this quarry that the fine Ancaster stone, used in the castle, was obtained (see Introduction, p. xv). The manor of Wilsford belonged to Lord Cromwell.

[4] Hesilburgh is in Northants; but this quarry was probably near Wilsford.

[5] Not known.

the 100; 13s.-4d. for 100 stones bought in the quarry of Asshby;[1] 5s.-5d. for 9 stones called perpont asshelers,[2] containing 36 feet, price 2½d. per foot; 2s.-8d. for 4 stones called fforme peces,[3] containing 8 feet, price 4d. per foot, bought at the said quarry of Hesilbargh; 4s. for carriage of the said stones called perpont asshelers and formepeces from the said quarry to Waynegate;[4] 5s.-10d. for 13 stones called odgyfes,[5] containing 47 feet, price 1½d. per foot, bought at the same quarry of Skowpe; 2s.-3d. paid to my lord's bailiff at Kyme[6] for ferry charges for carrying the said 460 asshelers from the quarries of Willesford and Hesilbargh at 6d. the 100; altogether £5-6s.-10d.

Carriage of stones

Cost of carriage of the same stones to the said castle, as is more fully detailed in the aforesaid quire, together with 13s.-1d. paid for the carriage of 110 freestones called sandston bought from John Kighley at the quarry of Salmondby,[7] etc. £8-13s.-9d.

Wages of masons.

Hire and wages of various masons engaged on the said works during the time of the account, namely Peter Mason, 12s.-8d., John Mason, £3-10s.-0d., Robert Mason, £7-9s.-11d., John Boteler, 13s., and £1-0s.-2d. for his 2 servants, John Mason of Waynflet, 4s.-8d., Robert Mason of Yorkshire, 5s. 6d. and Thomas Gemme, 5s.-6d. as is more clearly shown on the said sheet. £14-1s.-5d.

[1] The fine Carboniferous sandstone of Ashby-de-la-Zouch, from which the noble castle there is built, was much employed for superior architecture work. This stone was used also in the building of Kirby Muxloe Castle.

[2] Mr. Tipping explains this as meaning "stretcher stones for window panes"—*Tattershall Castle*, p. 66. Strictly, the word appears to denote a large ashlar stone throughgoing in the wall, so as to expose a dressed face on either side. Contemporary parallels for the use both of this term and of the words "form-pieces" and "ogives" will be found in the building accounts of Trinity College, Cambridge, 1428–31: see R. Willis and J. W. Clark, *The Architectural History of the University of Cambridge*, vol. II, p. 445, note 1.

[3] Pieces of tracery, wrought at the quarry.

[4] At Wainfleet.

[5] Ogival or ogee-shaped pieces of tracery.

[6] About 5 miles S.W. of Tattershall, across the Witham.

[7] Salmonby is 5 miles N.E. of Horncastle. The green sandstone from here was used for lining the base of Cromwell's new tower, as it is extremely resistant to water. As the enlarging of the moat round the castle, for which payments are noted *infra* p. 51, brought the bases of the ancient round towers into contact with the water, these also were cased with Salmonby stone.

Purchase and making of bricks called Waltile.

Cost of making, firing and carriage of 500,000 bricks called waltile made this year at my lord's brick kiln at Edlyngton More,[1] together with £11 paid in full settlement for the making of 550 of the same kind of bricks last year, as detailed in the same quire. £115-13s.-6d.

Cost of the purchase and carriage of bricks called waltile obtained from the issues of my lord's similar brick kiln at Boston,[2] as detailed in the same quire. £5-15s.-4d.

Wages of masons called Brekemasons.

To various masons called brekemasons and their servants engaged on different kinds of work at the same place for the period of the account, as is more clearly contained in the same quire. £50-13s.-10½d.

Wages of masons called Rughmasons.[3]

John Ramsey his mates and his servants called rughmasons, engaged in various jobs at the same place during the said time, as is particularly entered in the same quire. £15-15s.-3d.

Cost of quicklime.

Burning 10 kilns of quicklime for the said time, together with stones[4] and fuel bought for the said work, as is more clearly set forth in the said quire. £19-18s.-7d.

Purchase and carriage of timber.

Purchase and carriage of timber bought during the said time for the said works both in the Abbot

[1] Edlington Moor is 4 miles N. of Tattershall. The remains of the brick works may still be seen—a tangled wilderness of pits and ponds and spoil-heaps. The area covered is extensive, and comprises a round dozen or so of ponds, including two large ones. It is overlooked by Halstead Hall, a charming old brick house with Ancaster stone dressings on quoins, gables and voids. The house has four-light Perpendicular windows in pairs, a square-headed door with a hood mould in the centre of the front (looking S.W.) a four-centred arched door with a hood mould and shields in spandrels near the N.W. end, and a good plinth and a stringcourse at the first floor, both of Ancaster stone. The Hall is enclosed in a rectangular moat. Outside this, to the W., is a large barn, also in ancient brick, with diapers like those at Tattershall Castle. It has four-centred windows within square frames and hood moulds, all in brick. Halstead Hall has clearly been much altered in later times, but I see no reason why it may not represent the residence of Baldwin Dutchman. The kiln still standing at the derelict brick workings does not seem to be very ancient.

[2] References to Lord Cromwell's brickworks at Boston are frequent in the *De L'Isle and Dudley MSS.* between 1431 and 1452.

[3] Rough masons were builders of the foundations and rubble cores of the walls, as distinct from the freemasons who worked in dressed stone.

[4] I.e. limestone.

of Bardney's wood, £18-13s.-7d., and in Thornton[1] wood and elsewhere £4-18s.-10d., as appears in the same quire. £23-13s.-5d.

Cost of a chimney in the hall.

Renewing of a chimney made this year out of timber from my lord's wood at Elinton[2] during the time of the account, namely for the hall of the said castle, as is clearly contained in the said quire. £5-1s.-2d.

Carpenters' wages.

Various carpenters engaged on carpentry during the time aforesaid, as is set out clearly under their several names in the said quire. £14-18s.-4d.

Joiners' wages.

Robert Kerver[3] and his mate working on the ceiling[4] of the parlour and elsewhere at the same place and during the same time, as is more fully specified in the same quire. £2-14s.-3d.

Carriage of boards.

Carriage of boards during the aforesaid time: wages of John Fysher and others his mates as is particularly contained in the said quire 19s.-11d.

Palisading of the Castle ditch.

Carriage and making of a palisade on the counterscarp of the ditch on the west side of the castle, during the present year, as stated on the same quire. £2-0s.-6d.

Purchase and carriage of boards.

£7 for 200 boards called waynscott, provided by my lord at Hull, price of each 7d., carriage to Newdyke,[5] 10s.-5d.; £1-4s-6d. for 12 boards called plaunchers,[6] bought at Newerk, including carriage as in the same quire. £8-14s.-11d.

[1] Probably at Thornton by Horncastle.

[2] Ellington, 10 miles N.W. of Ripon, one of Lord Cromwell's Yorkshire manors.

[3] I.e. carver—a trade surname.

[4] It is possible that the word may mean panelling rather than ceiling. See J. H. Baxter and C. Johnson, *Medieval Latin Word List*, p. 72, under *celum*.

[5] See Curzon and Tipping, *op. cit.*, pp. 66–7.

[6] Planks or floor-boards, as distinct from wainscots for panelling. As the floor-boards are described as "bought", while the wainscots were "provided by my lord", it seems likely that the latter were foreign timber, "eastland boards" from Prussia perhaps. This supposition is rendered more probable because these wainscots were delivered at the port of Hull, a centre of commercial relations with the Hanseatic league and the Teutonic Order. The long hundred of 120 is used here.

Purchase of unwrought iron.

18 gaddes, 1 sheaf of osmondez,[1] 5 pieces of ffoldynyryn[2] and 2 pieces of iron chain called wyndowlandez,[3] bought for the same work during the period of the account, at various prices as more fully shown in the same quire. £3-17s.-9d.

Purchase of wrought iron.

Locks, chains, hooks, and such like small necessary iron articles, bought from John Loksmyth of Conyngesby[4] for the said work during the same period, as is particularly set forth in the same quire. 18s.-0d.

Iron-tools.

To John Smyth of Conyngesby, Ralph Smith, William Smyth and John Smyth of Tateshale for making various tools for the same work during the period of the account, as is more fully shown in the same quire. £4-0s.-6d.

Purchase of Nails.

8s.-6d. for 1,500 nails called great spikengs, 4s.-8d. for 1,400 nails called midilspikengs, 9s.-4d. for 4,500 nails called staknayle, 17s.-6d. for 14,000 latnayle, and 2s.-6d. for 3,000 latisnayle,[5] bought for the aforesaid work during the same period, as appears in the same quire. £2-1s.-6d.

Plumber's work.

£1-6s-8d. as a reward to John Plommer and his servants and 18d. to Walter Plummer, for various plumbing jobs and repairs at the same place, together with 10s.-3d. for 41 lb. solder for the same work, and 9s. for the wages of a certain man recovering lead from lead ash.[6] As in the same quire. £2-7s.-5d.

[1] A garb, strictly a sheaf or bundle, since used as a measure: a garb of arrows contained 24. Osmunds were bars of iron from the Baltic. They were "the very best iron used, and probably used only for the finest purposes, such as arrow-heads, fish hooks, the repairs of bell-gear, and the works of clocks". This iron was imported in short small bars, bundled into sheaves and packed in barrels. See *Proc. Soc. Ant. Lond.*, 2nd ser., vol. VIII, pp. 253–57.

[2] Presumably "folding" or "folden", i.e. folded iron. No doubt sheet iron is meant.

[3] I can offer no explanation of this word.

[4] Coningsby is the village next E. of Tattershall. John Loksmyth is evidently the same person as John Smyth of Coningsby in the next entry.

[5] Spikengs, large nails; staknayle, long nails for fastening stakes or posts; latisnayle, shorter nails for fixing laths or boards.

[6] *Cuiusdam hominis mundantis cineres plumbi.* *Mundare* means, strictly, to purge. Baxter and Johnson, *op. cit.*, p. 274, give, from a source *circa* 1250, *mundatio plumbi* "recovering lead from lead ashes".

Purchase of prepared glass.

£4-4s. for 112 feet of glass at 9d. and £1-0s.-0d. for 15 shields of glass at 16d. bought from Thomas Sturdwike of Boston for the windows of the parlour above the chamber and on the west side of the hall, as is more clearly set forth in the same quire. **£5-4s.-0d.**

Purchase and carriage of plaster

£1-16s. for 36 casks of plaster of Paris, 21 of them bought at Gaynesburgh and 15 at Granby[1] for the said work, price 1s. each; £4-6s.-7d. for carriage and £4-0s.-4d. for working this kind of plaster, as is particularly set forth on the same quire. **£10-2s.-11d.**

Carriage of bricks, sand, stone, and such like.

Wages of various carters with their carts carrying stone, brick, sand and such like for the same work for the aforesaid time, namely: John Bonour, £7-10s.-4d. for 180½ days at 9d. per day; Thomas Childe, £1-12s.-8d. for 49 days; Richard Baker, 11s.-4d. for 17 days at 8d.; and Richard Ermyt, 12s.-8d. for 38 days at 4d., as in the same quire. **£10-7s.-0d.**

Labourers' wages.

£1-17s.-6d. for Richard Sawer, £1-17s.-6d. for Robert Tiler, labourers hired each at £1-10s. per annum, that is for five terms falling within the period of the account; and £1-8s.-3d. for Robert Wilkynson and other labourers working on various jobs at the same place, as noted in the said sheet. **£5-3s.-3d.**

Scouring and emptying the Castle ditches.

Wages of Mathew Dyker and his mates scouring and emptying the water of the ditches round the said castle, namely, the wages of one man for 163 days beginning 28th March in the 13th year and to be continued until the first day in the close of the account,[2] receiving 5d. per day for piece work, as is made clear, in detail and day by day, in a certain sheet remaining in the hands of the accountant himself. **£3-16s.-3d.**

[1] Presumably Granby in Nottinghamshire.

[2] *Et continuandi ad primum diem in clauso compoti*, but I do not understand what is meant.

Purchase of boats and hire of boatmen.

£8-13s.-4d. for two boats bought by my lord in the month of December during the period of the account, for the purposes of transport in connexion with the said work, together with £1-19s.-4d., being the wages of John Drawall and other boatmen carrying in the same boats stone, bricks and other things needful for the said work, as also 12s.-9d. for other small purchases needful for the said boats, as is contained more fully in the said quire among the matters to be noted for the present account. £11-5s.-5d.

Pulling down houses at Revesby Abbey, etc.[1]

Cost of pulling down houses bought by my lord in the Abbey of Revesby during the period of the account, namely 6s. in wages of carpenters and other workmen, 1s.-9d. for hired carters carting 13 loads of timber, and 2s.-7d. being the wages both of my lord's servants and of hired casual labourers carting 11,360 bricks, 6 doors and 10 windows from the said houses, as is set forth in the quire. 10s.-4d.

Sundries

Various necessary outlays connected with divers works in the castle, incurred during the period of the account, as is detailed under two headings in the same quire, whereof the first contains £1-4s.-4d. and the second £3-11s.-3d. £4-15s.-7d.

Board of workmen

Board of various workmen engaged on the foresaid works in my lord's household between 15th February at the beginning of the account and the morrow of Michaelmas next following, as is set forth in the account of John Crakehall, clerk, at that time warden of the said household, closing on the same morrow of Michaelmas, so that he may have so much more allowed to him for the aforesaid board. £18-3s.-8d.

TOTAL £376-15s.-7½d.

[1] A Cistercian house 6 miles S.E. of Horncastle. Nothing of it now remains above ground.

Ditchwork and Scouring Ditches

Paid to Mathew Diker, hired to make anew 36 rods of ditch, beginning at the river Bain and descending in a straight line through the midst of Tateshale market as far as a certain temporary[1] gate called le Baryate—paid 1s.-8d. for each rod, conformably to a certain agreement made with him by Robert Gowshill, Rector of Cromwell. £3-0s.-0d.

To the same Mathew Diker, in part payment of £41-13s.-4d. granted him by my lord in respect of digging 210 rods of a certain ditch newly made, beginning at the said gate called Baryate and so descending as far as the east end of another ditch called le Newdike, for each rod 3s.-4d. £20-13s.-4d.

To the same Mathew for digging 340 rods of a new ditch called le Wardike on the west side of the above 210 rods, by my lord's command for each rod 5d.[2] £8-6s.-8d.

Carriage and making of hedges along the said ditch called le Wardike; 10s.-6d. to William Chapman and his mate for carrying 42 cartloads of willows from various places within the demesne of Tateshale, at 3d. the load; 7s.-6d. to Simon Lang and his mate for carrying 18 cartloads of thorns outside the park of my lord's chase at 5d. the load; 9s.-2d. to the said Simon and his mate for carrying 560 faggots called hegyng kiddes[3] from my lord's wood called Kirbywode[4] at 1s.-8d. for each 100; £1-13s.-4d. to William Peccham and his mate for new-making 340 rods of hedge along the said ditch called le Wardike, at 1d. the rod; altogether as in the aforesaid quire. £3-0s.-6d.

To the said Mathew Diker for enlarging and scouring 155 rods of ditch commencing at a certain gate called le Neweyate on the west side of my lord's close called Mikilhardclos as far as the sewer of the river Wythom, at 8d. per rod, conformably to an agreement made with him by John Fulnetby, along with 3s.-4d. granted to him as a reward by my lord. £6-0s.-0d.

[1] *Caducam,* "transitory", also sometimes means "frail", and here perhaps may signify "out of repair". For the work done under this contract, see Introduction, p. xii.

[2] It is curious why there should be so great a difference in the cost per rod of these three ditches.

[3] Hedging kids are bundles of sticks embedded in the bank on which a hedge is to be set, in order to give the bank consistency and stability.

[4] Kirkby-on-Bain, 3½ miles above Tattershall.

To John Pranke for making 30 rods of hedge called fotehegge[1] at various places along the said ditch, where it was most required owing to the overflow of water, at 1d. the rod. 2s.-8d.

TOTAL £41-3s.-2d.

Special allowances.

Allowed to the said accountant for the price of 1,160 faggots, being part of 15,124 faggots from the wood and underwood cut down in my lord's wood called Stikeswoldsouthwode, during the period of the account, but not allowed for above because they have not yet been used for firing bricks, but remain on the bank of the river Wythom; price 2s.-4d. the 100, as is acknowledged above, together with 7s.-8d. for cutting the said faggots, at 8d. the 100.[2] £1-14s.-6d.

Cutting 1,686 faggots belonging to the Prioress of Stikeswold, being the tithe of 16,800 faggots cut in the same wood, at 8d. the 100. 11s.-2d.

Paid to William Rokeray and his mate for cartage of the said 1,160 faggots from the said wood to the bank of the river Wythom, at 4d. the 100; the total is increased as a reward by 2d. by a certain agreement made by John Tailboys. 4s.-0d.

To John Warner, 18s.-8d. and to William Peper,[3] 12s. carpenters, in part payment of an old debt due to them by my lord, from the time when Robert Gowshill was overseer of the works of the said castle, by my lord's command, as attested in the account. £1-10s.-8d.

TOTAL £4-0s.-4d.

SUNDRIES

Parchment bought at Lincoln by Robert Broun for writing the present account, finishing on 15th February in the 12th year [of the reign]. 1s.-4d.

5 quires of paper bought both for detailing by the said accountant and also for writing out the present account, at 4d. the quire. 1s.-8d.

[1] A foot-hedge is a light dry hedge of thorns, planted along the outside of a quickset hedge to protect it during growth.

[2] *Marginal note:* the price of these faggots is held over until next year.

[3] In 1369 Robert Pepir was reeve at Driby, a manor of Lord Cromwell's, 4 miles W.S.W. of Alford (*Lincolnsh. Archæol. and Archit. Soc.*, vol. XXIII, p. 121). Possibly this William Peper was a descendant.

For 1 cartload of hay 2s., and 3 quarters of oats 5s., bought for the horse of the said accountant during the time of the account, together with 1s. for shoeing also reckoned in. 8s.-0d.

Personal outlays by the accountant riding on four occasions during the time of the account to Cromwell to obtain money from the rector there, 1s.-4d.; on another occasion in August riding to Boston to obtain and buy Spanish iron and to 6 chalders of coal, 5d.; on another occasion in December of the 13th year riding from Tateshale to Lincoln with a letter from my lord addressed to Sir[1] William Derby, canon of the Cathedral church there, 9d.; expenses of himself and John Warner going in October of that year to Kyme to choose out 20 oaks bought there by my lord for his hearth, 8d.; all of which amounts to 3s.-2d.

TOTAL 14s.-2d.

Accountant's salary.

At £2-13s.-4d. per annum, payable at the terms of Easter, St. Botulph,[2] Michaelmas and Christmas, as is allowed in the foregoing account, that is to say for five such terms following within the time of the account. £3-6s.-8d.

[ALLOWANCES]

Cash paid to the bailiff of Tateshale.

To Thomas Cowper, my lord's bailiff of Tateshale, the sum total of expenditure on divers works connected with his office, in excess of £19-6s.-2d. earmarked[3] as moneys received from the issues of the said office, as is clearly set forth in his account finishing at Michaelmas in the 13th year. £6-5s.-8d.

Receipt from the farmer of Snawdon

Similar sum delivered to the farmer of the demesne lands of Snawdon,[4] namely towards the cost of the ditch, by the hands of Mathew Diker £4, and of Baldewin Brekeman £2,[5] together with the

[1] *Dominus:* the usual courtesy title for a non-graduate clergyman.

[2] St. Botulph's day (17th June) is a usual rent day in Lincolnshire. It takes the place in this instance of the time of St. John Baptist (24th June).

[3] *Obstupatos,* literally "stopped up".

[4] I have been unable to find out where these lands were. From a later entry, see *infra* p. 73, it appears they were near Kirkstead. In 1443–44 Richard Grieve was bailiff there. See *De L'Isle and Dudley MSS.*, vol. I, pp. 208, 209, 210, 226.

[5] Matthew the dyker dug the ditch and Baldwin the brickman lined it with bricks, just as we see it today.

purchase of osiers for the same work, as on the same account finishing at the said Michaelmas. **£6-1s.-4d.**

Receipt from R. Leper.

Paid to Robert Leper, feller[1] of my lord's wood at Tumby,[2] 13s. 4d. for cutting faggots there, also £1 by the hands of John Kighley, as in the money received by the said John from William Stanlowe in January of the 13th year. **£1-13s.-4d.**

Receipt from J. Crakehall.

Paid to John Crakehall, clerk, late warden of my lord's household, for the price of various victuals, and other payments made on behalf of the said household by the accountant himself, as can be seen noted down in the said quire of paper, as also in the said John's account finishing on the morrow of Michaelmas. **19s.-9d.**

TOTAL **£15-0s.-1d.**

[*On the dorse*].

Sum of all the payments, expenses, allowances and deliverances above mentioned **£452-7s.-5d.**

Thus the remittances exceed the receipts above acknowledged by £19-19s.-6d. which will be allowed in next year's account.

RESPITES

£3-0s.-0d. advanced to Baldwin Brekeman for making 400,000 bricks not yet fired, by tally, on the account submitted, until the next account.

13s.-4d., whereof 10s. to John Swayne for 1,000 sheaves of thatching, and 3s.-4d. to William Forster in part payment of 8s.-4d. due to him for carriage of sand for the making of the said 400 bricks[3] etc.: to the next account.

£1.-7s.-4d., whereof 13s.-4d. for cutting faggots in the 2½ acres of wood bought from John Hert in the wood of Bardney; and 10s. to Thomas Lang of Conyngesby and his brother, and 4s. to William Borell for carriage of timber from the same 2½ acres of the said wood, etc., and so carried to respite for the next account.

[1] *Venditor bosci.* For *venditio* "felled wood", see Baxter and Johnson, *op. cit.*
[2] Tumby is 2 miles N.E. of Tattershall.
[3] *Sic*, in error for 400,000.

[£1-10s.-8d. whereof 18s.-8d. to John Warner and 12s. to William Peper, carpenters,[1] in part payment of an old debt due to them from the time when Robert Gowshill lately there was clerk of the works of the said castle, until such time as warrant is forthcoming.][2]

3s.-4d. to be paid to John Betson for the carriage of 28 boards called plaunchers from my lord's wood at Elinton, namely for their carriage from Lincoln to the ditch beside Tateshale called le Mersshedike, to the next account.

£2-5s. for so much money lying in the hands of Richard Frith, warden of the said household of my lord, in accordance with a composition made both with John Grene and his mate, in full discharge of £3 which he agreed to accept for felling and splitting 20 old oaks bought by my lord in the wood of Kyme, for fuel to be used in the said household, extra to £1 paid cash down to the said John, this is from the issue retained by the said Richard and not paid into my lord's coffer; as well as for a similar payment of 5s. to Richard Hieghage and his mate Thomas in the month of December of the 13th year, continuing 15 days burning charcoal in my lord's wood called Kirkbywode; getting 4d. per day at my lord's table; here respited until the next account.

RESPITED £8-19s.-8d.

Supplement showing respites totalling £27-8s.-6d., wherein are entered the names of creditors as per a bill containing £29-16s.-2d., and those are likewise debited as per receipt and payment from my lord's coffer.

Remaining in the accountant's hand £2-7s.-8d.

NAMES OF THE CREDITORS OF THE WORKS

Thomas Perch of Conyngesby, £1-6s. for timber and 5s.-8d. for nails bought from him for use in the aforesaid works, during the period of the account. £1-11s.-8d.

[1] *In parte* appears before *carpentarius*, by a scribal error in prolepsis for *in solucionis* following.

[2] The whole of the above entry, printed within square brackets, is stroked out in the MS and over it is written: "cancelled because allowed above". *See supra* p. 52.

John Lowys of Boston, for 11 gaddes of Spanish iron and 5 pieces of iron called faldynyron bought from him for the said works on three occasions.	£2-7s.-2d.
Roger Barker of Boston, 11s.-4d. for 3 gaddes of Spanish iron, and £1-4s. for the carriage of 6 chalders of sea-coal,[1] with £2-3s. for port dues on 12 chalders of the same coal and 2s.-3d. for port dues on 5,000 bricks, all reckoned together.	£3-19s.-7d.
Thomas Tilehouse for the carriage of 10,000 bricks from Boston to Tateshale in the months of December and April of the 13th year, at 1s.-4d. the 1,000.	13s.-4d.
Thomas Stoyle for carriage of stone, additional to £1 paid to him by the bailiff of Welby,[2] etc.	£6-1s.-8d.
John Betson of Lincoln for divers carriages to Tateshale, etc.	£11-9s.-9d.
William Forster of Stikeswold for carriage of faggots for my lord's brick-kiln, etc.	£1-2s.-2d.
John Warner, carpenter, for his wages in arrears.	£1-17s.-10d.
Thomas Toly, carpenter, in part payment of his fee.	2s.-0d.
Richard o' the Hill, carpenter, in part payment of his fee.	2s.-0d.
John Moller, in part payment of his wages.	2s.-0d.
John Thomson of Tumby for the carriage of one cartload of thorns.[3]	10d.
John Donour for carriage to the castle, etc.	6s.-2d.
SUM DUE TO THE CREDITORS	£29-16s.-2d.

[*Also on dorse, at other end.*]

[*On the dorse, at head.*]

The Account of Thomas Croxby, Supervisor of the Works of Ralph, Lord Cromwell at his Castle of Tateshale, finishing on the 2nd day of May in the 13th year of Henry VI.

Bricks of the smaller size made in the 10th year.

The undernoted accountant is answerable for 100,500 bricks of the smaller size called waltile made at my lord's brick kiln on Edlyngton More in the 10th year of the present king and still unused, that is to say, whereof each was of the size : length, 9 inches, breadth 4 inches, thickness

[1] No doubt brought by sea from Newcastle-upon-Tyne.
[2] A village 4 miles N.E. of Grantham.
[3] For the quickset hedge, see *supra* pp. 51–2.

2 and 4 parts of an inch,[1] as is more fully noted in the account immediately preceding. For bricks of this kind for the period of the account he does not answer because he received none of such a form, but only the larger size were made, as below.

Sum total, 100,500 whereof :

Abbot of Kirkstede.

The same accountant reckons there are due to be allowed to the Abbot of Kirkstede in respect of a greater number assigned to him by my lord, as the said accountant asserts without warrant, 35,400.

Abbot of Bardney.

And delivered to the Abbot of Bardney on the like assignation of my lord, in part of 20,000 by letter of warrant, 8,000.

And there have been laid out on divers works of the castle of Tateshale, by scrutiny of the books of the said accountant, 53,000.

Total sent, 96,400. There remain 4,100, of which at Tilehouse 2,300, at Merssbdike 1,800.

Bricks of the larger size made in the 11th and 12th years.

The accountant is answerable for 587,000 bricks called waltile of the larger size made in the 11th year, from those left over, whereof each is in size : length 10 inches, breadth 5 inches, and thickness 2½ inches, as appears in the previous account ; and of 550,000 bricks of this size made during the time of the account, as appears below : total 1,137,700, whereof :

The said Abbot of Bardney acknowledges.

The same accountant reckons that there are due to be allowed to the Abbot of Bardney on payment by my lord's order by Baldewin Brekeman as is asserted without warrant, 12,000. And there have been expended upon the works of the said castle, for the time of the account, as appears by examination of the account, 343,600.

Total dispatched, 357,600.

Remaining, 779,400, of which at the Tilehouse 529,400 ; at Mersshdike, 250,000.

[1] I do not know what subdivisions of the inch are here intended. In the castle today bricks of two sizes may be distinguished, measuring respectively 8½ by 4 by 2 in. and 7 by 3½ by 1½ in. The smaller ones are found mostly in the battlements.

II

13th April, 1438—31st May, 1439

Office of the Clerk of Works of the Castle of Tateshale. (Marg.)

THE ACCOUNT OF THOMAS CROXBY, SUPERVISOR OF THE WORKS OF RALPH, LORD CROMWELL, AT HIS CASTLE OF TATESHALE FROM EASTER, 13TH APRIL IN THE 16TH YEAR OF KING HENRY VI UNTIL 31ST MAY IN THE 17TH YEAR OF THE SAID KING, THAT IS FOR ONE WHOLE YEAR AND 48 DAYS.

Arrears.

He acknowledges £17-14s.-10½d., arrears from the last account, of the preceding year, as appears at the foot of the same.

TOTAL £17-14s.-10½d.

[RECEIPTS]

Cash received from my lord's receiver-general.

£251-0s.-3½d. received from William Stanlowe, my lord's receiver-general, by the hands of divers of my lord's servants in Lincolnshire and elsewhere, for the works of the said castle during the time of the present account, as is particularly contained both in the account of the receiver-general himself and in those of the aforesaid servants . . . from Michaelmas in the 17th year of the present king: along with £20 received from Henry Coote from moneys . . . of the wood and underwood of Tumby this year.

TOTAL £251-0s.-3½d.

Sale of bricks and faggots.

8s.-6d., being the price of 1,700 large bricks called waltyle sold to Roger Prestes this year at . . . 5s. the 1,000. £11-8s.-9d., being the price of 13,730 faggots cut this year in my lord's wood called Stikeswod S[outhwode] for use in my lord's kiln at Edlyngton, as detailed, price 1s.-8d. the 100.

TOTAL £11-17s.-3d.

Cash from my lord's coffers.

£47 received from my lord's coffer by the hands of various persons, namely: £6-13s.-4d. from John Croke on 13th June in the 16th year; £16-13s. .. .. .. from Richard W . . .[1] on two

[1] MS torn. No doubt Richard Westby.

occasions, first on the eve of Pentecost in the 16th year, £10 and secondly, on 29th August in the same year, £6-13s.-4d.; £20-6s.-8d. from John Tamworth on two occasions, first on the eve of Pentecost in the same year, £7, and secondly, on the eve of Easter in the 17th year, £13-6s.-8d.; and £3-6s.-8d. from William Stanlowe at Easter in the 17th year, attested in detail as above. £10-13s.-4d. received from the same coffers of my lord for Baldewyn Brekeman on three occasions, first from William Stanlowe at London, £5, and at Tateshale, £1, total £6; secondly from Richard Westby at Cheswyke,[1] £1-6s.-8d.; and thirdly from Peter Idle, £3-6s.-8d. £2 received from the same coffers for Godfrey Brekman at London on his first engagement and retention by my lord,[2] in part payment of £4 for his whole engagement by his indenture.

TOTAL £59-13s.-4d.

Discharged by creditors.

£2-15s. in cash from John Betson, a creditor of this business both last year and this, discharged in respect of a certain . . . payment of cash owing to him by my lord, out of the mere and proper acknowledgement of the accountant of this account.

TOTAL £2-15s.-0d.

SUM OF THE WHOLE RECEIPT, INCLUDING ARREARS £343-0s.-9d.

Surplus from the last account.

For the preceding year, as appears at the foot thereof. £11-12s.-4d.

BUILDING EXPENSES AT THE SAID CASTLE

Various outlays incurred in respect of the works at the Castle of Tateshale during the whole time of this account, as is detailed in a certain quire of paper prepared for this account, which has been carefully revised, and remains among the memoranda thereof.

[*Stonework.*]

Freestone purchased, £8-9s.-7d. Carriage thereof, £8-19s.-4d. Quarrymen's wages, £22-7s.-2d.

[1] There is a Cheswick in Northumberland, near Berwick, but I do not know if this is the place.

[2] This suggests that Godfrey, like his chief Baldwin Dutchman, was a foreigner who came to London on Lord Cromwell's invitation.

[*Brickwork.*]

490,700 . . . [bricks] called waltile made by Foys Brekmaker, £69-5s.-1½d. Cash paid to Baldewyn Brekmaker for making 8,000 of such bricks, £17-16s.-4d. Carriage of the said bricks made by Foys Brekmaker, £21-10s.-2d. Purchase of such bricks at my lord's kiln at Boston, with their carriage, £4-0s.-10½d.

[*Masons' wages.*]

Wages of masons called brekmasons £47-1s.-2d. Wages of John Ramsey and his mates called roughbrekmasons,[1] £18-13s.-10d.

[*Ditchworkers' wages.*]

Wages of Matthew Dyker and his mates digging a foundation for le countremure, the great stable and other houses there,[2] £29-11s.-6d.

[*Quicklime.*]

Cost of making quicklime, including purchase of stones and charcoal, with carriage, £42-16s.-5d.

[*Timber.*]

Purchase of timber in the wood of the Abbot of Bardney, with carriage, and carriage of suchlike timber from the wood of Braunceton,[3] £22-5s.-8d.

[*Carpenters' and sawyers' wages.*]

Carpenters' wages, £35-4s.-6d.; sawyers' wages, £2-6s.-4d.

[*Miscellaneous purchases.*]

Spanish iron, £4-19s.-9d.; making of tools therefrom, £4-12s.-7d.; nails, £3-12s.-2d.; glass, 9s.; plaster of Paris (including carriage), £10-0s.-3d.

[*Labourers' wages.*]

Wages of labourers, £5-4s.-8d., inclusive of board, and £10-1s.-8d. for carrying bricks, lime, sand and suchlike from the water[4] into and outside the castle.

[1] Brick masons were able to lay the "purpose-moulded" bricks, while rough brick masons were employed only in the main masses of the walling.

[2] The countremure is the revetment wall on the outer side of the ditch. The great stable still remains in the Middle Ward.

[3] Branston, a manor belonging to Lord Cromwell, 3½ miles S.E. of Lincoln.

[4] No doubt from the Bain, up which these materials would have been brought (see next entry).

[*Miscellaneous.*]

Purchase of boats for my lord, wages of labourers transporting materials with the said boats, £2-12s.-8d. Purchase of necessaries for the works within the castle, £2-12s.-4d. Cost of baling all my lord's wool within the said castle, apart from £1-15s. paid by Elias Warde, £7-3s.-5½d. Making and scouring ditches in various places, £16-9s.-2d. Making of hedges and fences in various places, £5-1s.-6d. Costs incurred at the Manor of Whitehall,[1] 10s.-2d. Minor necessary outlays, £4-10s.-4d. Purchase of lead and casting thereof, £5-13s.-8d.

TOTAL AS SET FORTH IN DETAIL ABOVE £434-1s.-4½d.

SALARIES AND WAGES

Salary of the accountant in respect of his service for a year, as is allowed to him in the preceding account, £2-13s.-4d. His wages for 21 weeks, from 27th June till 12th December, both within the period of the account when my lord's household was at Colyweston,[2] in addition to 2 weeks in September when he was at the charge of my lord's household abroad, and also 1 week in October at the time of the baling and weighing of my lord's wool, when he was at the charge of my lord himself, for each week 1s. as he was accustomed to have, £1-1s. And for the like wages of the said accountant on two occasions when my lord's household was away at Whithall, on the first occasion for 4 weeks, 4s., between 20th February and 1st April, besides 1 week when he was at board with my lord's auditor; and on the second occasion between 24th April and 1st June,

[1] The "Tower on the Moor". See Curzon and Tipping, pp. 63–64, also *infra* p. 79. All that now remains of this is an octagonal stair turret at what was the N.W. corner of a rectangular tower, with an annexe of thin walls, evidently later, to the N. On the W. face are two loopholes in two chamfered orders, the inner pointed, the outer four-centred. On the S. face is a square-headed window with double-hollow chamfer on jambs and head and a single broad chamfer on sole, all in Ancaster stone. Near the top of the turret on the N. side is an arched loop with a single chamfer. The turret has a brick plinth. It has contained a brick stair, now broken down: its steps were carried on ascending arches. The brickwork in Old English bond closely resembles that at Tattershall, but has fewer burnt ends and no diaper. The wall head of the main structure on the N. front shows the springer of a corbel arcade. Four doors from the main structure into this stair, with chamfered brick arches, survive. The annexe shows two small aumbries close together, one with the springer of its arch. The track of a fosse is still evident round the tower.

[2] A manor of Lord Cromwell's in N. Northamptonshire, near Ketton. Here also he built himself a house and here he died, on 4th January, 1446.

for 5 weeks within the period of the account, 5s., at 1s. per week as above, during which time my lord's household was at Whithall, 9s.

TOTAL £4-3s.-4d.

CASH EXPENDED

To William Stanlowe, my lord's receiver-general, to be paid to John Irlond, steward of my lord's household,[1] for 60 karffs[2] of peat bought at Swyneshed Fen,[3] £1; for their carriage thence to the ditch beside the cemetery of the church of Tateshale, by water, during the month of January in time of the account, 4s. Board and reward of two men from Wymondham in Norfolk, staying at Tateshale to make faggots in my lord's wood called Frithkarhage,[4] for the said household, in February and March, 10s.-8d. Wages of several men collecting 60 cartloads of dry fuel in the wood of Myntyng[5] at 2d. the load, 10s. with carriage of them thence to Tupholme[6] dyke £1, and from there to Tateshale by water, 19s. Wages of John Drawall and his mate carrying 30 quarters of malt from Braunceston to Tateshale, 2s.; also carrying 25 quarters of oats from Boston to Tateshale for the use of the household in November, 2s. Cutting of fuel in Tateshale Chace for making charcoal for the said household, 6d.[7] Paid to John Kent for making and burning the said fuel, for 26 days in October and November, 8s.-8d. Making and carriage of 6,490 faggots from Frithkarrhage, to be used in the said household of my lord,[8] at 13s. 4d. the 1,000, £4-6s.-8d.: altogether, as detailed above. £9-3s.-6d.

[1] The word *Standardi* follows here, but I cannot explain it. In the fifteenth century it sometimes signifies headquarters, and this may be the meaning here.

[2] I have not met this word elsewhere. Perhaps it simply means "carved" or cut pieces. Opposite this entry in a later hand is the marginal note: "note for the old church of Tattishall". No doubt by this the parish church is meant, as distinct from the new chapel in the castle.

[3] The Cistercian Abbey of Swineshead, now a farmhouse, is 6 miles S.W. of Boston. It was here that King John took the famous "surfeit of peaches and cider" which caused his death at Newark on 19th October, 1216. Shakespeare makes John die in the orchard of Swineshead Abbey.

[4] Unidentified.

[5] Minting is close to Stixwould.

[6] The remains of the Premonstratensian Abbey of Tupholme may still be seen about 7 miles N.W. of Horncastle.

[7] Charcoal stoves were evidently used in the living rooms. A marginal note has been added here: "Likewise, £2 9s. for getting and carrying dry fuel, in its own proper allowance and not to be charged to the said steward of the household".

[8] Again the mysterious word *Standardi*.

To the said Receiver-General, to be paid to Peter Idle, Steward of my lord's household abroad,[1] for the making and carriage of 300 heaths in Tateshale Park in August, because of my lord's arrival there, 1s.-8d.[2] Wages of John Drawall for 11 days in August and September, carrying with a boat, bread and ale from Boston to Tateshale for use in the said household, at 4d. per day, 3s.-8d. Making and carriage of 300 faggots called ellerkiddes,[3] from the aforesaid coppice at Frithkarr', for use in the said household, 4s. Altogether, as set forth in detail above. 9s.-4d.

William Stanlowe, Receiver General, accounts for the above total in his account for this year.

TOTAL £9-12s.-10d.

SUM TOTAL OF THE ALLOWANCES AND PAYMENTS £459-9s.-10½d.

Surplus.

£116-9s.-1½d.; besides 9s.-6d. for the making of 1,490 faggots in the aforesaid coppice called Frithkarr in April last year, for use in my lord's household[4] in the time when Gilbert Knaresburgh was Warden thereof, at 8d. the 100. And thus he has surplus of £116-18s.-7½d.

RESPITES

15s., being the price of 3,000 bricks sold to John Weende[5] last year, which he says my lord has forgiven him. Therefore respited until the accountant can speak with my lord. £3-15s.-10d., being £2-13s.-4d. from the salary of the said Thomas Croxby for a whole year ending at Easter in the aforesaid 16th year, and £1-2s.6d. from that of Richard Sawer for three quarters, with an additional sum due of £1-10s. per annum, in respite by order of my lord until the accountant can speak with him.

TOTAL RESPITED £4-10s.-10d.

v.

There is charged to Roger Barker, my lord's bailiff at Boston, for the price of 6 chalders of

[1] *Forinseci.* This may mean simply, not in the manor of Tattershall. It seems to be contrasted with the word *Standardi* applied to the other household.

[2] I can only conjecture that heather-beds are meant.

[3] Bundles of faggots made from elder.

[4] *Standardi.*

[5] Lord Cromwell's overseer of works in Lincolnshire.

sea-coal which he says he has released for use in the lime-kiln of the said castle which the said accountant denies having received at that time. Therefore again charged against the said Roger, at 5s. the chalder. £1-10s.-0d.

[*Dorse.*]

Sum total of allowances.

Less surplus, £466-0s.-2½d. Which having been allowed and deducted, brings out a surplus of £122-19s.-5½d. From which sum has been received, from the issues of my lord's manors in Lincolnshire, since the closing of the accounts at these, in the aforesaid 17th year, as noted in detail below, £51-9s.-5d. These sums having been deducted, the current surplus is £71-10s.-0½d. For which sum are shown the names of creditors amounting in all to £81-15s.-10d.

[CREDITORS.]

Names of the creditors because the accountant has reckoned again in next year and . . . as well as those creditors others particularly.[1]

John Mason	£1-4s.-0d.	John Loksmyth	£2-13s.-4d.
Robert Mason	13s.-4d.	Ralph Smyth	£1-12s.-0d.
Godfred Brekmason	£2-0s.-0d.	John Drawall	1s.-6d.
Matthew Brekmason	£2-0s.-0d.	Robert Clerk	8s.-0d.
James Brekmason	£1-17s.-0d.	William Borell	16s.-0d.
Cristine Brekmason	£2-3s.-0d.	John Swyne	10s.-8d.
John Ramsey	£1-0s.-0d.	John Prentys	8s.-8d.
John Warner	£1-6s.-8d.	John Flixburn	£1-5s.-7d.
William Pepir	£1-0s.-0d.	Henry Plummer	7s.-2d.
Richard Grebby	10s.-0d.	Parson of Ingoldmells[2]	£2-6s.-8d.
John Sleght	£1-4s.-0d.	John Kighley	£1-0s.-0d.
Thomas Botiller	7s.-2d.	John Sawer	£1-2s.-0d.
William Loode	6s.-6d.	William Levely	£1-15s.-10d.
William Danby	3s.-4d.	Abbot of Kirkstede	6s.-8d.
Thomas Toly	2s.-0d.	John Hert	£3-13s.-4d.
John Perche	7s.-6d.	John Betson	£28-16s.-0d.
William Sawer	£1-15s.-0d.	Richard Palmer	3s.-0d.
John Chambour	4s.-0d.		

[1] MS torn and sense imperfect. The list of names has been cancelled. On the right margin is noted the total £81 15s. 10d.

[2] Ingoldmells, a coastal parish N. of Skegness.

John Freston[1]	3s.-0d.	Richard Swyne	£3-6s.-8d.
William Peecham	3s.-4d.	John Borell	£3-6s.-8d.
John Bonour	£1-13s.-10d.	Robert Trewlofe	4s.-4d.
John Thomson	18s.-0d.	Thomas Tumby	1s.-8d.
Edward Ussher	£1-0s.-0d.	Robert Tyler	6s.-0d.
		Foys Brekmaker	4s.-4d.
		John Lowys	£4-8s.-1d.
		John Docheman	10s.-0d.

[*At other head of dorse.*]

Receipt acknowledged of 247,900 large bricks remaining over from the preceding year: also of 490,700 large bricks made this year, as below, by Foys Brekmaker at the same price; and of 8,900 similar bricks bought this year, as below, from John Chamberleyn, lessee of my lord's kiln at Boston, both due in arrears and in payment of his rent.

TOTAL, 747,500 bricks.

From the foregoing bricks, it is estimated that there will be required for the masonwork of le countremure within the Castle of Tateshale, made by Mathew Brekman and his mates as below: 182,000. On the new building of a large stable within the Castle, at the west end of le Wolhous, by Godfrey Brekman and his mates, within the period of the account, as below:[2] 236,000. On the foundations of a small house between the aforesaid stable and le Wolhous, made by the said Godfrey Brekman and his mates, as below: 46,000. Sold, as below, to Roger Preestes of Horncastle, from my lord's bricks in Edlyngton More: 1,700. On the mason work of my lord's mills at Tateshale: 25,000. Given from my lord's alms for the works of the fabric of the Church of Edlyngton: 3,000. Used in various other works within the said Castle, such as the repair of partitions in the chimneys and in the market house, delivered by the workmen day by day and not by the thousand, by estimate for the number of days' work: 114,000. For the chimneys and windows of the said stable, of the worked bricks called hewentile:[3] 2,200.

TOTAL: 619,900 bricks.

There are left over 137,600 bricks, whereof at the disposal of Baldewyn Brekman there remain to be accounted for, at the kiln, out of the whole amount of bricks unaccounted for there last year, 134,600; within the Castle, 3,000.

[1] Doubtless a native of Frieston, a village not far distant.

[2] Note particularly that Matthew Brickman and Godfrey Brickman are actually in charge of the building of these considerable works, just as their chief, Baldwin Brickmaker or Brickmason, appears to have been in charge of the Tattershall building undertaking as a whole.

[3] "Purpose-moulded" bricks.

Faggots. 15,260 faggots cut this year in my lord's wood called Stikeswold Southwood for use in my lord's kiln at Edlyngton More as below.

From which are given in tithe to the Prioress of Stikeswold, in respect of faggots cut this year, as above, 1,530. And felled,[1] as below, for use in my lord's aforesaid brick kiln, on the admission and under the oath of the accountant, 13,730.

Summed as above, and balanced.

III

Welby, 29 September, 1438—29 September, 1439.

By the hands of Thomas Croxby, Clerk of Works at Tateshale Castle, £3-3s.-7d. for the purchase of freestone for the works of the Castle ; 14s.-10d. for the carriage thereof from the quarry to Appiltrenesse.[2] TOTAL £3-18s.-5d.

By the hands of Thomas Croxby for 35 cartloads of plaster of Paris from Londonthorp[3] to Appeltreness for the works of Tateshale Castle, on several occasions, £2-1s.-0d.

[1] *Vendicio* here means "felling". See Baxter and Johnson, *op. cit.*, p. 450.

[2] On the river Slea in the neighbourhood of South Kyme. In 1315 it was said at an inquisition that Ewerby and Ewerbythorpe ought to repair and maintain the south side of the water called Apiltrenesse unto Kime—W. Dugdale, *A History of Imbanking and Drainage*, 1672, p. 228.

[3] In Kesteven, N.E. of Grantham.

IV

31st May, 1439—27th March, 1440.

The Account of Thomas Croxby, supervisor of the works of Ralph, Lord Cromwell (at his Castle) of Tateshale aforesaid from the last day of May in the [18th] year of the reign of King Henry VI . . . until the Easter following on the 27th March next thereafter following, for 300 days.

Arrears.

The said Thomas acknowledges £6-0s.-10d. of arrears from the last account as is noted at the foot thereof. £6-0s.-10d.

[RECEIPTS.]

From my lord's Receiver-General.

£353-1s.-8¾d. from William Stanlow, my lord's Receiver-General by the hands of various servants in Lincolnshire for the works of the aforesaid castle, during the period of this account, as detailed both in the account of the Receiver-General himself and also in the accounts of the said . . . servants ending at Michaelmas in the 18th year of the present king. Also £3-15s. from the . . . Receiver-General, by the hands of Robert Gowshill, clerk, Receiver for the counties of Nottingham, Derby and Leicester, for the price of 25 carts of plaster of Paris from the issues of the demesne of Granby,[1] and sold to the said accountant for the aforesaid works, as appears in the account of the said receiver under the head of . . . £356-16s.-8¾d.

Sale of bricks, faggots and peats.

12s.-6d. for the sale of 2,500 large bricks called Waltyle, sold to various persons this year, price 5s. per 1,000. For faggots, used this year for hedgerow enclosures and for firing bricks in the kiln, for which there is no receipt, because there was no felling[2] of my lord's faggots, but so many came by purchase. But account must be made for £2-13s.-4d., price of 60 carffs of peat from those peats which were bought from Kesteven Fen by the same accountant last year, as sold by him to John Dokkynge of Whaplode by his acknowledgement on the account. £2-5s.-10d.

[1] A Nottinghamshire manor of Lord Cromwell.
[2] *Vendicio* here = felling.

Sale of barley and old timber.

£14-7s. for the sale of 37 quarters 5 bushels of barley received from my lord's granary by the hands of Richard Sawer the keeper thereof, that is to say, coming from this grain from the parts of Norfolk before Easter within the period of this account, at various prices, as set forth under the present year in the detailed account book of the said accountant. £3-6s.-8d. from William Plummer of Lyn. . . .[1] for old timber from a house there bought by my lord from the said William and so sold to him [William] by the said accountant. £17-13s.-8d.

Cash from my lord's coffers.

£7 from my lord's coffers, by various hands: from Mathew Dyker and William Stanlowe £1; from Richard Westby on two occasions, £3; from Baldewyn Brekmaker, £2 and John Mason, £1, in full and due acknowledgement of the said accountant upon this account. £6-17s.-8d. from the said coffers by the hands of Ralph Harple, clerk, my lord's receiver in the county of Norfolk . . . moneys paid into the hands of Richard Flynt in the month of March in the said 18th year of the reign of our present king. £8 received from the said coffers by the hands of the said Richard Flynt for so much money received in a certain bag of the said accountant, Thomas Croxby . . . after the feast of the Purification of the Blessed Virgin Mary in the 18th year aforesaid. £4-2s-6½d. from the said coffers by the hands of John Lowys of Boston, at Tateshale in March of the aforesaid 18th year. £26-0s.-2½d.

From John Weende.

Receipt for £4-8s. from John Weende, being the price of 2,200 faggots bought by him from John Gedney and others at Horsyngton[2] for use in my lord's brick kiln at Edelyngton More, price 4s. the 100, as set forth in more detail in the account of the said John Weende closing at the feast of St. Valentine previous to the termination of this present account. £4-8s.-0d.

[1] Possibly Kings Lynn (at that time Bishop's Lynn), but the MS. is torn here. As the only letters visible are Lyn this could equally well be Lincoln.

[2] Four miles W. of Horncastle.

Charging of new creditors.

Receipt for £6-8s.-10d. from Richard Flynt for payment of certain creditors of this office, whose names, with the sums due to them, are set out in detail in the account rendered by the said Richard and filed along with this and the other accounts. Also receipt for £53-8s. from the surcharge of the new creditors for the whole period of this accountant touching the office of the Clerk of Works at the Castle of Tateshale, the names of whom, with the sums due to them, are set forth separately. £59-16s.-10d.

TOTAL INCLUDING ARREARS £473-2s.-1d.

Surplus.

From which there is reckoned as surplus from the last account for the preceding year, as set forth in the foot thereof. £122-19s.-5½d.

BUILDING EXPENSES AT TATESHALE CASTLE.

Various outlays incurred in respect of the works at the Castle of Tateshale during the whole time of this account, not only by the accountant himself but also by Richard Flynt, as set forth in detail in a certain quire of paper in respect of this account submitted and carefully examined and remaining in the memoranda, with £45-1s.-8½d. paid by the said Richard Flynt, my lord's auditor, between Christmas of the 18th year aforesaid and Easter next thereafter, at the close of this account. £320-0s.-10d.

Rents of the manor and grange of Marton,[1] etc.

Paid by the said Richard Flynt to the Prioress of Staynefeld for the rent of the manor and grange of Marton in full payment for the year ending on the Feast of St. Philip and St. James in the 18th year of the present king, reimbursed in terms of a quittance, £3-9s.-5½d. Also moneys paid by the said Richard Flynt to John Howson of Conyngisby in part payment of £1 expended by him for two parcels of meadowland bought from him and included within a certain new enclosure of my lord beside the mill of Tateshale, in addition to 16s.-8d. paid by the said Richard to the said John and allocated in a certain account made by the said Richard between Easter in the 18th

[1] Martin by Horncastle.

year aforesaid and the feast of St. John the Baptist, next thereafter, filed in the same file, 3s.-4d.

TOTAL £3-12s.-9½d.

Extraneous expenses.

Repaid to Roger Barker, my lord's bailiff at Boston, for 6 chalders of sea coal,[1] which he says he expended on the lime-kilns of the said castle, but the said accountant denies having received these, so the sum is recharged on the said Roger, to wit £1-10s.-0d.

Roger Barker, bailiff of Boston, in his account at Michaelmas, in the 18th year of the present king, acknowledges under the heading of external receipts, this sum of 30s.-0d.

SUM TOTAL OF ALL MONEYS ALLOWED AND PAID £448-3s.-1d.

Sum total owing £24-19s.-0½d.

RESPITES.

15s. the price of 3,000 bricks sold to John Weende in the 2nd year preceding, which he says my lord forgave him. This matter to be held over until my lord has been consulted. £3-15s.-10d., wages of the said Thomas Croxby[2] for a whole year ended at Easter, in the 16th year of the present kind. To Richard[3] Sawer for three quarters of the following year, being due £1-10s. per annum in respect of my lord's order for so long. £13-8s.-9d. paid to Baldwin Brekmaker for making and firing bricks called Waltyle in Edlyngton More for the works of the said castle, additional to those which, as specified on the dorse of this account, are already expended on the said works. Not yet used therefore in suspense till delivered. To the same, £1-19s.-7d. . . . the price of 120 boards called Weynscotes, part of 300 such boards bought at Skegnesse by John atte Hall, junior, bailiff of Candelesby, for the works of the castle of Tateshale, besides 2,100 of the same boards delivered this year for the works of the said castle and allowed for above in the details of the buildings—in suspense because they are not yet delivered but remain at Ingolmels in the house

[1] *I.e.*, true coal, brought in by sea, as distinct from peat or charcoal.

[2] £2 13s. 4d. is written in over the name.

[3] xxii is written in over the name and the figures following are lost. The amount was probably 22s. 6d., three quarters of 30s.

of Thomas Lowys, as is asserted by the said John atte Hall.

SUM OF THE RESPITES, CARRIED OVER	£19-19s.-11d.

and there remains in addition on the said Thomas Croxby, accountant, clearly . . . £4-19s.-10½d.; which sum, indeed, the said accountant Thomas acknowledges above, under the heading. *Receipts from my lord's coffer*, with £8 found in his purse as indeed, which £8 appears there . . . are his private property as set out below.

[*In dorse.*]

NAMES OF THE CREDITORS.

John Mason [*Whereof all paid by John Weende* (Marg.)	(8s. 8d.)c
Robert Thymelby, mason *Whereof paid* 6s. 8d. (Marg.)	iiis ivd (10s.)c
Godfrey Brekmason	£1 10s.
Matthew Brekmason *Whereof the whole paid by the same John* (Marg.)	(17s. 8d.)c
James Brekmason	£1 8s. 8d.
Christian Brekmason *Whereof the whole by the same John* (Marg.)	(£1 16s. 8d.)c
The wife of John Dauber *Whereof paid* 6s. 8d. (Marg.)	vs ivd (12s.)c
Thomas Botiller	3s. 4d.
John Perche *Whereof* 10*s. paid as above* (Marg.)	iiis iv (13s. 3d.)c
William Sawer *Whereof* 13*s.* 4*d. paid as above* (Marg.)	xs (£1 3s. 4d.)c
William Grabye *All paid* (Marg.)	(4s.)c
John Loksmyth *Whereof* £1 13*s.* 4*d. paid* (Marg.)	vis viiid (£2 0s. 0d.)c
Ralf Smyth *All paid* (Marg.)	(4s. 2d.)c
Robert Clerk of Boston	8s.
John Hert	£2 0s. 0d.

William Borell'	4s.
Henry Plommer	2s.
John Flixburn	2s. 6d.
John Betson *All paid by the same John Wende* (Marg.)	£24 17s. 2d.
Richard Swyne *Whereof paid 6s. 8d.*	iiii £3 6s. 8d.
John Borell' *Whereof paid* 13*s.* 4*d.* (Marg.)	ii iiis ivd (£2 6s. 8d.)[c]
Thomas Stoyle	6s. 8d.
John Roper *All paid as above* (Marg.)	(1s.)[c]
William Wodeson *All paid as above* (Marg.)	£1 0s. 0d.)[c]
Agnes Besyngham of Kyme	3s. 4d.
John Toynton	2s. 6d.
William Peccham	3s.
John Swyne *All paid* (Marg.)	(4s. 8d.)[c]
John Bonour *Whereof 6s. 8d. paid as above* (Marg.)	xis (17s. 8d.)[c]
William Rokerey *All paid* (Marg.)	1s. 8d.
William Levely	3s.
John Lowys	£1 14s.
William Holwel *All paid* (Marg.)	(1s. 4d.)[c]
William Fissher *All paid* (Marg.)	(£1 3s. 4d.)[c]
William Ablet	4s.
The Abbot of Kirkstede *All paid* (Marg.)	(£1 10s.)[c]
John Chambr' *Whereof paid 3s. 4d.* (Marg.)	is viiid (5s.)[c]

£53 8s. (Marg.)

BRICKS

The undernoted accountant accounts for 137,600 large bricks from last year's surplus; also for 474,500 bricks made this year by Baldewynn Brekmaker at the same price, likewise of 24,000 large bricks bought this year, as below, from John Chamberleyn, lessee of my lord's kiln at Boston, both in respect of arrears and as his rent for the current year. TOTAL 636,100 bricks.

From which he reckons will have been used for the paving of the great stable and the building of the supports thereof[1] on two occasions both by days and also by thousands as vouched for by the carriers, 28,500. Also used in the new building of a wall of one house situated between the stable and the mill-house, both as above and also by thousands as vouched for above in the present account, 48,600. And in divers other works at the said castle, for example in renewing the walls, raising the two galleries and likewise walls of the castle at the end of the kitchen and its chimneys and elsewhere in many works carried out on a daily basis, as by estimate both in this way and also by the sworn testimony of the said carriers 2,095,900 bricks. Sold, as below, to Edmund Ussher (1,000) and Thomas Rudde (1,500) from my lord's bricks at Eddyngton More, 2,500. Given to the Abbot of Kirkestede, on my lord's order, this year, 5,000.

TOTAL 4,080,500.

There remain 355,000 bricks, whereof 134,600 are at the disposal of Baldewÿn Brekmaker and 121,000 for the new ditch at the castle.

FAGGOTS

9,000 faggots bought this year as below from the Abbot of Kirkestede, both from Brakenwood (4,000) and from Highawe[2] (5,000), by knowledge of the accountant. 2,200 bought this year, as below, from the feoffees of William Ratheby, 880 of such faggots bought this year, as below, at Thorneton Wood, 400 faggots bought from the Vicar of Stixwold this year, as below.

TOTAL 12,480.

From which have been used in fences round the great enclosure between Snawdon and Kirkestede, 5,000: in fuel for my lord's kiln at Edlyngton more by knowledge and oath of the accountant, 7,480. TOTAL AS ABOVE: BALANCED

[1] *les ponyons*. The medieval Latin word is *punzunus*, which properly signifies a puncheon or timber strut. Here presumably the brick base of such is implied. Possibly the meaning is "sleeper-walls"; but no such remains are now visible in the Great Stable. On the other hand Mr. F. L. Salzman explains the word "pynnyon" in the Tattershall College contract of 1486 as meaning "gables"; see his *Building in England*, p. 545.

[2] Bracken Wood and Highall Wood are just N.E. of Woodhall.

V

25th March, 1445—25th March, 1446.

The account of John Southell, Clerk of the Works for Lord Cromwell of the Castle and Demesne of Tateshale from Lady Day in the 23rd year of Henry VI to Lady Day following.

Arrears. £25-8s.-2d. from the previous year's account, as set forth in the end thereof.

RECEIPTS.

£440-4s.-4d. from Robert Wymbissh,[1] my lord's receiver in Lincolnshire, i.e. from the issues of his office for the year ended Michaelmas in the 24th year of the reign, as is more fully set out in the said Robert's account, £1-7s.-6d. from Henry Etwall,[2] my lord's receiver for the shires of Nottingham, Derby, Leycester and Stafford from my lord's issues of Typeshelff[3] for carriage of lead from the Peak[4] to Lincoln, as more fully set out in his account.

TOTAL £441-11s.-10d.

Extraneous sales.

£2-10s.-5d. for a pipe of old red wine sold by the accountant from my lord's cellar at his order in the May of this account, 11s. for an iron stithy remaining for a long time with my lord and now sold to Ralph Smyth, 10s. for 2,000 large bricks sold to the Warden of Tateshale College.

TOTAL £3-11s.-5d.

TOTAL RECEIPTS, WITH ARREARS £470-11s.-5d.

Surplus: from the last account, £2-12s.-8d.

BUILDING COSTS.

For the new-building of the plantation ditch,[5] and for other buildings and works at the Castle of Tateshale, at Whithall and elsewhere: Free-

[1] Wimbish is a village in Essex, near Saffron Walden.

[2] Etwall is a parish 6 miles S.W. of Derby. Lord Cromwell had important landed interests in this county.

[3] Tibshelf, near Alfreton in Derbyshire.

[4] The lead mines in the Peak district have been worked since Roman times. In the fifteenth century they belonged to the Crown, as part of the Duchy of Lancaster, and were leased to farmers. See *V.C.H., Derbyshire*, vol. II, p. 330.

[5] Presumably a brick-revetted ditch—no doubt the ditch enclosing the pleasance (see plan, Fig. 1).

stone masons, £50.-0s.-7d., Brick masons, £73-12s.-9d. Carpenters, £38-12s.-11d. Purchase and carriage of freestones, £30-12s.-3d. Expenses on the brick kiln, with purchase of fuel and carriage thereof by land and water, £86-10s.-6d. Labourers' wages, £60-17s.-2d. Carriage of timber, faggots, stone and coal by water, £6-5s.-11½d. Sawyers' wages, £10-10s.-11d. Expenses on the lime kiln, with purchase of coal and fuel,[1] £15-8s.-11½d. Purchases for the works of the castle, £6-19s.-8½d. Cost of the ditch and its enclosures,[2] £6-13s.-4d. Purchase and manufacture of iron tools, £13-8s.-2d. Purchase of freestones called sandstones for the buildings at Whithall and Burwell[3] and for the marsh called le Syncarr,[4] £13. Plumbers' wages, with carriage of lead from the Peak to Tateshale, £5-7s.-6d. Purchase of rope for the works, £6-17s.[5] Purchase, carriage and mixing of plaster of Paris, £8-6s.-10d. Purchase of bows and arrows and cleaning of harness in the castle, £4-12s.-3d. Baling of wool and other materials, in the wool-house, £2-2s.-1d. The accountants' board and wages, with board and wages of Robert Tyler for the period of this account, as is more fully detailed in a sheet of paper completed thereafter and lodged for this account; it is kept in the bag containing the accounts for the year, £5-7s.-4½d.

TOTAL	£446-6s.-3d.
Sum of all the said allowances	£448-18s.-11d.
And he owes	£21-12s.-6d.

RESPITES

£15, the accountant's fee due for four and a half years ending at Easter in the 23rd year of the reign, at £3-6s.-8d. per annum. £11-16s.-8d. of

[1] *Focale* here evidently means wood as distinct from coal.

[2] I take it that *sepacis* must be meant for some word akin to *sepis*, hedge, fence, enclosure.

[3] Burwell is 5 miles S. of Louth. There seems to be no other record of Lord Cromwell building here. Probably he was assisting some work at the Benedictine Priory of Burwell, an alien house which at this time was in a poor way and before 1464 had been granted to Tattershall College (*De L'Isle and Dudley MSS*, vol. I, p. 199). The last Abbot on record died in 1427, when it was found that "the site of the priory with dilapidated buildings was worth nothing beyond repairs".—*V.C.H.*, *Lincs.*, vol. II, p. 238.

[4] For this pond, see Curzon and Tipping, p. 64. It still bears the name, and is in the parish of Roughton, S. of the Tower on the Moor.

[5] No doubt the rope was required for tying the scaffolding poles.

the sum paid to Baldwyn Brekemaker for the making and firing of bricks called Waltyle at Edlyngton More for the works of the said castle (excluding other bricks specified in the dorse of this account and delivered for the works of the said castle), because the [first mentioned] bricks have not been delivered.

TOTAL RESPITES £26-16s.-8d.

From which those liable are in the next years' accounts under the heading " arrears ".

Carried forward to next year's account.

From the above, excluding the said wages deducted from the total sum due, the accountant finds himself with a surplus of £5-4s.-2d., from which he charges £5-14s.-2d. against the creditors, as below.

CREDITORS.

Peter Martyn, 3s.-10d.	Phineas Blyncasope, £1-1s.-0d.	
Thomas Ratheby, 2s.-10½d.	John Conns, 2s.-2d.	
Peter Dyker, 13s.-4d.	John Hert, 13s.-4d.	
Thomas Plommer, 5s.	John Enterpath, 9s.-7d.	
John Cowper, 6s.-8d.	Thomas Godefrey }	£1-2s.-4½d.
William Ablot, 14s.	Thomas Lauerans }	
	TOTAL	£5-14s.-2d.

[Dorse.] The account of John Southill, Clerk of the Works at Tateshale Castle ending on Lady Day, in the 24th year of the reign of Henry VI.

BRICKS

The undermentioned Baldewyn Brickmaker for 284,000 bricks received from the remainder of last year. 383,000 large bricks made this year by the said Baldewyn of the same value as the last lot supplied for the works of the said castle and the repair of my lord's house in Tateshale and otherwise during the period of the account, 84,000 small bricks made by the said Baldewyn and supplied this year as above.

TOTAL, 741,600.

Whereof it is reckoned that 322,000 of the large size will be used in the great tower called le Dongeon and other minor works of the castle. For the making of a new contremure on my lord's instructions at the head of the Syncarr, 94,000 large bricks. Sold to the Warden of Tateshale College for the new-making of an apartment in the house of John Warner 2,000 large bricks, given by my lord to the Provost of Edlyngton Church for its rebuilding, 5,000 large bricks.

There remain 318,600 whereof 100,000 large bricks and 84,000 small bricks are on the bank of the new ditch : in all, 184,000, and in Baldewyn's hands, arrears of old standing, 134,600.

TOTAL, 423,000.

VI

Account of Richard Parker, bailiff, for the year ending 29th September, 1472.

For the whole year finishing at Michaelmas in the 12th year of King Edward IV.

Repairs done to the Castle.

Henry Dente, carpenter, for making two new bridges, himself and two assistants, for 80 days, each at 1s.-4d. a day. . . .[1]

Thomas Sawer and his mate, for carriage of timber, by agreement, in gross, 10s.

Thomas Colynson, labourer, for assisting the carpenters and for digging, 12 days' work at 4d. a day. . . .

William Colynson, similar work, 15 days at 4d. a day. . . .

John Smyth, labourer for similar work, 4 days at 4d. a day. . . .

Richard Graybe and John Rayburne, carriage of 33 cartloads of timber from Grubholme[2] to the castle, at 3d. the load. . . .

Thomas Caton and Richard Graybe, carriage of 14 cartloads of timber from the park to the Castle, at 4d. the load. . . .

William Smyth for 110 large nails for the great bridge . . . beside my lord's outer stables[3] . . .

Henry Dente, carpenter, for repairing the horse mill. . . .

The said Henry and John Wode, miller, for cogs and spindles bought for the horse mill. . . .

William Horner, tiler, for repairing the kitchen chimneys, 3s. . . .

The same, for repairing the oven hearth in the bakehouse, 22s. . . .

Carriage of two cartloads of clay for the above repair. . . .

Thomas Nevyle, tiler, 12 days' work at the Castle. . . .

The same, for taking down bricks at the Tower on the Moor, 5 days' work at 6d. a day.[4] . . .

1 bunch of stonelath[5] nails bought from Richard Leverton. . . .

8 ridge tiles[6] bought . . .

3 quarters and 1 bushel of lime, at 1s. the quarter. . . .

William Kelsey for a wheelbarrow for use in the Castle. . . .

TOTAL, £9-7s.-6d.

[1] The remainder of these items, where marked with a dotted line, have been destroyed by damp.

[2] I cannot identify this place.

[3] In contrast to the *magnum stabulum* in the outer ward.

[4] This important entry tells us that the Tower on the Moor was already so called in 1472, and that at that time it was being despoiled to provide bricks for repairs at Tattershall Castle.

[5] Nails used to fix slates or tiles to the parking of a roof.

[6] Tiles covering the ridge of a roof.

INDEX OF PERSONS AND PLACES

INDEX OF SUBJECTS

* Page numbers are given for the Latin text only.